Antidote to
ANXIETY

Antidote to ANXIETY

A ROAD TO FEARLESS FAITH

KATIE B. SMITH

Antodote to Anxiety
A Road to Fearless Faith

Published by Lucid Books in Houston, TX
www.lucidbookspublishing.com

Katie B. Smith
Atlanta, Georgia
http://carefullycareless.org

ISBN: 978-1-63296-466-3
eISBN: 978-1-63296-465-6

For the constancy of little boys,
which keeps me from overthinking life.

CONTENTS

Prologue

A ntoinette Portis' children's book, *Not a Box*, was a fan favorite in our home. My four boys loved the box design story, but all kids love the concept of pretend no matter the medium. Sadly imaginations are quickly fossilizing in our screen-filled, voice-activated, instantaneously-answered world.

Curiosity once killed the cat, but now, anxiety is her silent threat. Without an outlet for creativity or critical thinking, imaginations quickly turn to fearful frets and anxious worry. It is no secret that an increasing number of our population—both youth and mature—is clinically or self-diagnosed with anxiety disorders. I believe we all possess an innate desire to calmly create, and our imaginations don't cease to exist when we enter adulthood. We have just made it increasingly difficult to think on what is true, noble, and lovely because there's a plethora of already-created material right at our finger tips.

As someone who suffered from severe anxiety as a child and into young adolescence, I know the pitfalls and panic that surround palatable fear. It is real, but there is also a real path towards fearlessness.

One of the key components of increased anxiety is too much time to think, or using what little time we have to think on the wrong things. Our modern advances, coupled with social "scrolling," give us too much time to think on things that add unwarranted worry to our already jam-packed lives. When we stop learning, playing, trusting, and serving, our imaginations turn to darker things. Yet, there is light and hope to be shared. I hope to share some of those good words here. Through truthful **saturation**, meaningful **service**, and humble **silence**, we can finally **settle** ourselves and regain fearlessness.

Anxiety in a man's heart weighs him down, but a good word makes him glad (Proverbs 12:25).

1

Starting fearful

"Avoiding danger is no safer in the long run than
outright exposure. The fearful are caught as often
as the bold."

— Helen Keller

*H*eart pounding. Sweaty palms. The voices of others
played on fast-forward as I watched helplessly off screen.
Everything sped up, yet I was slowly trudging through
jello, trapped in shaky unsynchronized shell-shock. I wanted
to crawl into the fetal position and be rocked to sleep, hoping
it was a terrible nightmare. Unfortunately, this was another
"normal" panic attack driven by fears and anxiety, but why?
I wasn't even old enough to spell anxiety let alone figure
out where it originated. My family nucleus consisted of two

loving parents and two happy siblings. There was no one in my peripheral struggling with fear. My mother and father were notably the most self-assured individuals in our entire sphere of influence. I always followed in-step with the familial extraverted enthusiasm, but various environments set off a sort of consternation that debilitated my youthful joy.

ࣣ֌ࣦ

I remember it vividly. Everyone was clearly "over-acting" and playing up the excitement around the first day of school. With shaking sobs, I was not falling for their farce. An old video-recording shows two children delighted about an upcoming adventure, and one very distressed child preparing for the gauntlet.

After my refusal to enter the school bus, which I rode the entire two years prior without any issues, my mother reluctantly drove me back to Braden River Elementary School, hoping for a hug and a hand-off. My self-employed, self-controlled, and self-starter parents could not be persuaded by any negotiations let alone yield to any hysteria. Thus, my arm was forced into my second-grade teacher's hand as I frantically screamed watching my mother's back exit the building.

Because my hysterics disturbed the rest of the building, I was immediately taken to the counselor's office. I implored the woman to let me call my mom as if I were being held hostage. "You cannot call your mother until you calm down," she sternly replied. Having been sobbing for nearly two hours at this point, I was struggling to comply with her demands. In an agitated attempt to control my nerves, I accidentally ripped off the three-dimensional flower I had been gripping on my shirt. Now, I feared I might be taken to an insane asylum for apparel abuse. This single nervous action quickly altered my sobs into stiff peaks of silent panic.

The school counselor then conceded to call my mom, and while I held the flower strategically in place, I tried to reason with her. I would do anything and everything to learn from the comfort of our home, but what I heard come out of my mother's voice changed my tune. I worshipped my mom, so when she spoke, I listened.

My mom left her home at the age of eighteen without batting an eyelash. She also didn't like to show emotion unless it was a universal symbol, so when shaky vulnerability began to permeate her vocal cords, I was shocked. Her tired tears traveled through the phone line. "I don't know what to do Katie," she balked. "You have to go to school." My always-composed caretaker seemed as desperate as I was to finish this phone call, but her momentary fragility actually aided in our future resolution.

Like a toddler two-step, it was suggested that my mom work from the school "work-room," which was across from my classroom. I could check for her presence during every class break or hallway ritual, and little by little she could show up less and less until I "forgot to look." While this was effective for a time, my parents eventually conceded to follow the "safe and secular" route (visiting a psychologist) in dealing with my anxiety, which began to surface outside of the school walls.

ෘාෆ

My juvenile experiences may be amplified due to time and perspective, but they are pertinent to the topic of anxiety because, however moderately they compare to others, they were a very real part of my upbringing and my character. I worshipped and idolized people like security blankets. Those blankets shifted from person to person as time passed. Yet today, any one of my childhood friends or family members would not recognize the person I have become. My security and stability are not wrapped around another human being or my own perceived control because of the drastic fears and realities I was forced to face. Like many, the hard parts of my life threw off those soft, fuzzy blankets, exposing the rough edges of reality. But instead of hardening my heart, those situations actually taught me the *antidote to anxiety*: "whatever is true, whatever is noble, whatever is right, whatever is pure, whatever is lovely, whatever is admirable—if anything is excellent or praiseworthy—think about such things."[1] My control lied only in my thoughts and my time, which if left unchecked, would spiral into a vicious cycle of angst. Yet, with such limited perception of an invisible world, I needed to learn "the peace of God, which transcends all understanding, and would, in fact, guard not only my heart but also my mind."[2]

While I do not claim to have any degree or license in psychology or emotional/mental disorders, I do know about life stressors that lead to fear and anxiety. Before delving further into remedies or transformations, I must pause and denote the differences that exist between "clinical anxiety" and "biblical anxiety" in order to affirm those situations that are beyond my understanding. Without humility, you begin to exact absolutes that only exist in biblical truths, not societal standards caused by sin.

2

Alternate anxiety

"I have learned over the years that when one's mind is made up, this diminishes fear; knowing what must be done does away with fear."

— Rosa Parks

Pride has a way of muddying the water. What should be clear and simple becomes cloudy and grey because you confound processes with presumptions. In other words, stiff necks only harden hearts. When there is only one right path towards well-being, we dangerously draw conclusions that either nullify or trivialize the experience of someone else.

However, let me clarify that these statements by no means negate absolute truth. Quite the contrary, relativism, like pride, also generates ambiguity in that without an absolute truth, we are in the muddied water of contradictions.

There may be only one path towards Heaven, but how we find that path looks very different from person to person. Two plus two always equals four, yet one child may learn mathematics best through visual depictions and another through tactile placements. Likewise, our stories are all written differently, but there is still one creator of storytelling, even when we respond to those stories differently.

Personality tests, enneagrams, and other assessment indicators were created to help people identify their learning styles, but not everyone can fathom truth in the same way. People don't typically tell children about sex, drugs, and murder at the age of three, but that doesn't mean they lie to them either. We explain truth in a way that kids can comprehend. Likewise, if someone is taught from infancy only to believe in things he/she can see, then the truth of God may not penetrate their heart until it softens and the layers are peeled back. When someone says, "There is no such thing as absolute truth," that person is actually making a statement that he or she believes to be absolutely true—a contradiction or self-defeating statement.

> "You'll remember that when people believed in God as the source of ultimate truth, they depended on the *revelation* of His will as the basis for what they would believe and how they would act. But the more people relied on — and glorified — reason, the less they relied on revelation, until they had forgotten about it completely. You see, revelation can't be

proven. You can't see God or touch Him. You can't hear His revelation audibly, so scientists began to say that it didn't exist. [Moreover,] scientists have some pretty good ideas about how dinosaurs lived and moved. They base these ideas on the evidence found in fossil records, bone structure, organic deposits, etc. But there comes a point beyond which scientists can't prove anything, because they can't replicate the creatures and experiment on them directly. So they just have to believe what the strongest evidence suggests. There is no difference between that faith and the faith we place in God and the Bible, as long as that faith is founded on the best facts we can find."[3]

Think about absolute truth as the trunk of an ageless tree, while viewing anxiety and depression as the various branches growing in different directions. When we presuppose that there is one way to eradicate all anxiety, we make outcomes more complicated by neglecting the shady branches or the ones shriveled from drought. Specific choices dictate the direction that the branches grow, but a single trunk holds them all in place. We should examine both the trunk and the branches in order to grow away from fear and anxiety. All those branches look the same, but they have chosen different paths affecting their ultimate outcome. In other words, making the grand statement that medicine should never be used to battle anxiety and depression ignores those times when a medical prescription allows someone to get back to square one in order to absorb truth. Some individuals are too befuddled to even read words let alone absorb their significance. However, once they've silenced their spiral of self-talk, they are able to step into the reality and comfort of absolute truth.

We also should not presume that once a problem has been erased through medication, that it is something to merely rely on when life is hard. Every story has a different plot, but if we desire the outcome of freedom from fear, we must do the hard work of humility and grace along the way. We can keep water clear or coffee black without all the added "opinions." My story to fearless faith is just one of many.

As I share my own pilgrimage towards "fearless faith," I am not posing an absolute prescription for the masses, but presenting an individual route towards emancipation that may aid others in their process.

&CB

When I use the term "clinical anxiety" I am referring to the realm of a medical condition affecting the thoughts and emotions that can lead to various physical symptoms. The American Psychological Association defines *anxiety* as "an emotion characterized by feelings of tension, worried thoughts and physical changes like increased blood pressure."[4]

The National Institute of Mental Health includes a long list of possible side effects caused by general anxiety disorder (GAD) including fatigue, muscle tension, difficulty concentrating, irritability, restlessness, and sleeplessness.[5] The introduction of anxiety often leads to *panic attacks*, which NIMH also correlates with heart palpitations, nervous shaking and shortness of breath. Furthermore, NIMH claims a panic attack creates more fear than the actual fear itself: "People with panic disorder often worry about when the next attack will happen and actively try to prevent future attacks by avoiding places, situations, or behaviors they associate with panic attacks. Worry about panic attacks, and the effort spent trying to avoid attacks, cause significant problems in various areas of the person's life."[6] Strictly speaking, it's a vicious cycle of angst trapping many people today.

According to the ADAA, at least 40 million adults suffer from some kind of anxiety, and 6.8 million of those are actually diagnosed with GAD.[7] This doesn't even take adolescents or children into account. Besides, when we naturalize terms, like "worry," we run the risk of creating relationships where both parties are harmed. Those who actually suffer from anxiety are fueled by the commonality of those who normalize "worrying," and commonality creates desensitization.

Not realizing that worry and anxiety are biblically interchangeable, fellow "worriers" don't see a need to actively change or grow in their struggles, while those with actual mental disorders are carrying weights larger than their backs can brace, crippling and collapsing their creative purposes. We must be careful, then, how we define such struggles, or casually use such terms in everyday conversations.

American pastor, author, and speaker David Platt defines the term "biblical anxiety" as it relates to the vocabulary consistent with Greek and Arabic usage. He states in a sermon/ podcast:

> "We need to be careful not to read our definition of 'anxiety' into the 'biblical' use of the word [because]

Jesus commanded his disciples 'not to be anxious,' then those who suffer from clinical anxiety might think to themselves 'is my medical condition a sin?' When the reality, as best as we can tell, is that Jesus isn't referring to a medical condition [in the book of Matthew]."[8] Platt then notes that the word is also used in conjunction with positive forms of genuine care and concern, as when the biblical author, Paul, expresses his love for the church of Philippi and Corinth using the same term that we label "anxiety."[9]

Thus, Platt prodigiously defines "biblical anxiety" or biblical worry as "**carrying concerns in this world in such a way that we lose *perspective* on life and/or lack trust in God.**" When you lose your *perspective* or trust by trying to be God yourself, then the weight of the world inevitably pushes you into panic.

What then can be done if biblical anxiety sprouting from sinful control turns to clinical anxiety with physical ramifications? First, you must humbly accept your place in the world because none of us is God. Even when you acknowledge this fact mentally, you may not practice it literally. Instead, you hold a tight grip on your plans. Changing your course midstream is not even an option in your rule book. You make up your mind about people, places and personal affects without room for error or recalculation. You decide what is best for you and your family because you would only choose what is best, therein neglecting the time needed to reconsider your motives. You use "always" and "never" as if you are in charge of those domains.

After, acknowledging your place below God, next, seek to pinpoint what you are fearing or fretting. Often times this must accompany the trained ear of a counselor or some type of clinical conversation. Whether it's a therapist, a licensed psychologist, or even a deeply trusted friend, the first step in moving past a problem is to identify it. No matter your level of self-awareness, advice stemming from encouragement always brings an increased level of comfort. "Anxiety weighs down the heart, but a kind word cheers it up"[10]. You are given communities and companions to encourage, rather than discourage you, and as you grow spiritually you can receive extensive solace from the Holy Spirit Himself. A wise psalmist identifies with this: "When anxiety was great within me, your [Lord] consolation brought me joy"[11].

For me, at eight years of age, I was no where near spiritual maturity, and my encouraging parents knew I needed professional guidance in hopes that I'd receive lasting comfort. We began the journey with a child psychologist...

3

Safe and secular

"Do the thing you fear, and the death of fear is certain."

— Ralph Waldo Emerson

What do you see when you look at this? After World War II, Hermann Rorschach developed the "ink blot test," which became widely popular among clinicians for various studies of the human psyche. "When used appropriately, the Rorschach uniquely reveals a person's level of energy, control of emotions, and thought processes."[12] In other words, modern science and the Bible both teach that our lives are moving in the direction of our thoughts. *"For as He thinks in his heart, so he is"*[13] (NKJV). How you view interrelationships between people and environments acutely influences your thought-life, which in turn affects anxiety levels. It would appear that whether you are speaking of biblical or clinical anxiety, the world agrees on the theory that *perspective* is everything.

"But do not overlook this one fact, that with the Lord one day is as a thousand years, and a thousand years as one day."[14] *Perspective* matters. Whether you're sitting down with an infamous Swiss psychologist staring at ink blots or an educated Christ-follower like Pastor Platt, "Carrying concerns in this world in such a way that you lose *perspective*" provides the concerted core of any issue causing fear.

∾⟊∾

Just two weeks after starting second grade, the school counselor agreed with my parents that a visit to a child psychologist might be helpful. Those ink blots are a bit blurrier now than they were in person almost two decades ago, but I do remember being asked the question: "What do you see when you look at this?" In my case, the Rorschach test didn't solve the riddle of origin, but it did give insight into my issues. After one or two sessions, it was concluded that I was dealing with emotional thoughts too advanced for my age. Even though my parents had a healthy marriage at the time, I was fearful of losing my mother to divorce, death, or some other dreadful ordeal. My parents were encouraged to enforce reality, not fearful fantasy, to offer constant reassurance, and finally to look into an advanced placement option (gifted class) at school in hopes of redirecting mental stimulation appropriately. To this day, I still cringe at the phrase: "It's all going to be okay," because I attribute those words to my parents "reassurance tactics." I certainly had a rattled state of mind, but I already knew (mentally not practically) that everything would likely "be okay." I wanted to stop the fears from surfacing, and the placation felt particularly superficial. I wanted to get to the root of the problem, but I guess that's what everyone wanted to no avail.

Parents are in the constant reassuring business regardless of a child's natural disposition, but words without correlating action only heighten uncertainty. As the adage states: *more is caught than taught.* Well, my parents taught like professionals. I owe more gratitude and admiration for their loving guidance than words can accurately express. However, I caught many a lesson on self-reliance and independent strength, which equipped me to try my hand at headship instead of *perspective.* When you must "toughen up" in preparation for life, you teeter on hubris; staking claim on your life might produce strong leadership skills, but later it can pressure pack you into an unexpected panic attack.

Knowing that both my parents were the first in their families to attend college gives a little insight into the pressure they must have felt themselves. Whether it was intended or perceived pressure, my mom and dad chose to transform their potential angst into ambition. This is probably one of the safer modes of dealing with intensity, but like any volcano, eventually that self-inflicted force will need an exit strategy, and oftentimes it's not an easy exit. My parents also firmly believed in mental strength, which they were taught (or caught) by their parents. We didn't take medicine for every ache and pain, and we were told that our power to control our thoughts was critical in directing emotions. While I thoroughly agree that our minds have incredible, untapped potential to control thoughts and emotions keeping anxiety at bay, we must also set that reality up against the knowledge of God and our position toward Him. "[You can] demolish arguments and every pretension that sets itself up against the knowledge of God, and [you should] take captive every thought to make it obedient to Christ".[15] Therein lies a huge weapon of the mind in maintaining *perspective*, yet it's not always clear how to take those worrisome thoughts captive. If you are setting yourself up to be "god," then your thoughts may also grow at an exponential rate, requiring you to survey a range of emotions in hopes of preparing for the unexpected. Again, you are pressure-packing yourself to the point of eruption.

‘’

My parents "eruption" didn't begin letting out steam until a couple years after my ink-blot test. At first my new "target" classes at Braden River Elementary provided thought-provoking stimuli that initially aided in my transition to second and third grade. With just a handful of students, we were given space to debate, critically evaluate, and artfully analyze grand topics like rescuing endangered animals and solving mathematical word problems from more than one angle. The freedom from rote memorization was intoxicating and kept me from needing any pharmaceutical aids or medications, which my parents would probably have denied either way. However, any spare time seemed to make my thoughts wander again and remind me of what fear tasted like. The fear that I might have another panic attack at any moment caused a restlessness I didn't know how to control. I remember wandering down the halls one day in a desperate search for my big sister. I thought that if I could just see her face, just know someone from my family was nearby, and fill her in on my tension, she'd somehow become a security blanket and calm my nerves. Even if she had never been my antidote in the past, I'd hoped her two additional years ahead of me might give her some consoling discernment.

She saw me banging on her classroom window and embarrassingly shook her head in confusion. Her teacher, who was confined to a wheelchair, eventually had to roll to the door and ask if I was "all right." After seeing how much effort she put into disrupting the entire class, I felt even more estranged when my sister had no words of wisdom. I was left to focus on my previous apparel abuse and risk the counselor's office, or move forward to what I'd seen my parents achieve in moments of stress. I definitely returned to class and tried a new approach to control my thoughts because I feared alienation more than anything. *I was safe, and I could do anything I put my mind to do.* Unfortunately, this secular-mode of prideful thought put me on a path toward more lies and fictional fears that I could not have predicted. There is increased pressure when you are queen of the future holding all the power in your two little hands.

New York pastor and theologian, Tim Keller, once said that living in this world without succumbing to its detrimental mindset means **"God will have to take you out of your power to revive you. If you build your life on anything**

27

besides God, you will live in fear"[16] You will be scared of the polls, scared of the market, scared of the mirror, and in my case, scared of losing the security I needed from someone I loved.

I was learning to let off steam through self-control and self-awareness, but this brought a new form of "control" that would not serve me well towards my freedom from fear. *Perceived power was hindering my progress.* Moreover, my previous psychological exam proved prophetic in many ways. My family unit would soon explode sending us all in different directions. When your perceived power directs your steps, you have to put blinders around your eyes like a horse pulling a carriage. You cannot look to the left, to the right, or behind you, because you may miss your opportunity to move ahead. While blinders help keep animals and humans from jumping into sudden shock, they can't be worn at all times without stupefying the host. You begin to neglect realities in your tunnel vision, which can cause marital strife, disregard for responsibility, or personal neglect.

In the case of my parents, their professional achievement agendas occurred at the expense of their marriage (this is not to say there weren't many other contributing factors, as most broken families understand: there are layers of love and hate to rummage through in order to accurately recall what was added to fan the flames). Flawed humans create flawed fires, and when you are overwhelmed with new flames, you naturally look for cover or a "band-aid." Like a child, you want anything to cover up the scrape so that you don't have to see it bleed.

4

Facing Fears (not band-aids)

"Not everything that is faced can be changed, but
nothing can be changed until it is faced."
— James Baldwin

*H*ave you ever seen a child lose his grip while climbing?
Even if he is aware that you are right there to catch him,
he instantly starts crying or screaming. This reaction
stems from fear: fear of falling, fear of getting hurt, fear of not
being caught, or fear of the unknown peril that awaits. We all
share this reaction into adulthood. But if we believe that there
is always someone there to catch us, then why the impulsive,
automatic response? Because it is a natural response to
potential harm. We are conditioned to brace before blunder;
this basic instinct benefits mankind (most of the time). If we

didn't clench and prepare for the worst or scream for help, our bodies may endure more harm as a result. Thus, it's an advantageous reaction when it protects our body, but when it hinders our spirit from facing fear, it loses its value.

I'm under the assumption (albeit true or false) that people don't want to be victim to worthless thoughts, wasted time, or unwanted distractions from what they deem truly valuable. But since everyone values various aspects of culture differently, no one agrees on the best avenue to pursue. Instead, we must be pushed, literally, to fall in order to escape the opposing paths that falsely blind us. An increasing number of remedies to escape anxiety, health problems, or moral decay, beyond just spiritual guidance, exists in our culture today, but people have become more and more jaded by the "rules of religion," turning their efforts to practicality. I would argue that the "rules of the world," not faith, hold us all in captivity. *Eat this, watch that, take this many steps, sleep this many hours, DIY this way, invest here, buy there.* It's exhausting and causes so much unneeded anxiety for so many men and women, especially in western culture.

However, when you actually ask God, the creator and sustainer of simple joy to rid you of all unnecessary preoccupations, you must be willing to fall into the unknown and even scrape up your knees along the way if you hope to become fearless and free from anxiety. Don't confuse *simplistic, faithful* choices with *easy, foolish* choices. Simplicity requires simple, hard steps. You must be open to endure the hard in order to achieve long-lasting results in the letting go of your instincts, because not all instincts are beneficial. Moreover, you can't get to a place of pure fearlessness on your own designed recipe; your innate self-preservation will cause you to scream for help or cover up the scrapes without cleaning the wounds. When God has handed me something hard, it's only when I've embraced it instead of avoided it that I've been able to recalibrate my attention correctly and rise above it. This is what the Biblical author, James, meant when he said, "Consider it pure joy whenever you face trials because you know that the testing of your faith produces perseverance. Let perseverance finish its work so that you may be mature and complete, LACKING NOTHING"[17] (emphasis added). You especially won't lack *perspective* if you let the hardship finish its work. Although, if you put a "band-aid" on the pain, you may not achieve the perseverance that leads to perfection (lacking nothing), which ultimately gives you that profound joy from seeing it through to the end.

Unfortunately, different types of "band-aids" all serve the same purpose: cover up the hurt. When something is too agonizing to endure, you grab the band-aid readily available, or one that you have witnessed working for others. A sedative, a stimulant, a sip of something, a screen, or sensuality, all aid in distracting you, like a popsicle for a child's complaint. These distractions might be harmless at first, like that icy cold treat, but if you indulge further, then one popsicle becomes ten for breakfast, and now you have entered into dangerous territory.

Cyclical sin spirals you into lifestyles that are merely subconscious, survival habits. You have to brace yourself to rip off the band-aid and see how deep the cut really goes. Hopefully, it's still at the surface, and the infection hasn't spread, but there are situations that require amputations in order to fully repair the limbs.

ುಗ

My family moved to Georgia when I was nine, my sister was eleven, and my brother was six years-old. The first year involved a normal adjustment period, but what I remember most about that year was the horrible nightmare I had that my parents were getting a divorce. They hadn't shown a single disagreement in front of me or my siblings, so I confessed my fears from a great level of shock. Staring strangely at one another they reverted back to their reassurance strategies from two years prior, explaining that it was simply a dream. Needless to say, they were separated the next year, divorced the year after, and my dad remarried the following year. The aftershock hit us all differently, and thus, everyone grabbed different band-aids to soak up the mess. Between the five members of my family nucleus, the methods of mending mutated over the years. Fortunately at the time of the wound, I was moving into middle school, and merely shifted my worship of my parents to that of my friends. As God would have it, I met a variety of people inviting me to a variety of after-school activities, which helped me feel more stable and secure at the time.

Over the course of my awkward adolescence, I was stirred in a melting pot of *perspectives,* but the freedom to think gave me tools to find authentic faith for myself. I attended Wednesday night confirmation classes with a friend at her Catholic Church, participated in Discipleship Now at a friend's baptist church, frequented an Episcopal church and a methodist church for familial nostalgia, visited Friday morning Fellowship of Christian Athletes in high school and Saturday

Jewish temple celebrations, as well as learned from atheist, agnostic, and super "spiritual" friend groups. Moreover, I was invited to pot-smoking parties, co-ed sleep-overs, and many more "all-inclusive," inexhaustible arrays of self-indulgence. All the while, my ever-present apprehensions and anxieties actually aided in my balance and naiveté. I avoided extremes and unknowns out of fear, thereby protecting myself from detrimental delinquency. However, I believe most of the counterbalance credit goes to an unseen Father directing my steps towards fearless faith.

∞∞

My panic attacks subsided for a while as I focused much of my self-controlled energy into "keeping the peace" among my fractured family. I didn't realize it at the time, but seeking to serve or think of others first in survival mode actually gave me needed (albeit stressful) purpose. Once I had made my silent peace with the structure of our family (while continuing silent prayers for amicability among everyone), I began centering my security blanket around everything that was within my control, my calendar, and my comfort zone. My predictability was priceless, even to the point of becoming the butt of many jokes.

As my home-life was less stable, I was able to sleep away from home more easily. As siblings wandered away, I was able to walk with independent confidence; all the while believing lies that I could control my future, which I was still very afraid of not knowing. I was afraid of not having enough money, getting sick, being betrayed, and even missing out on something. I feared things I couldn't explain while trying to stabilize everyone so that there was never any pain, sorrow, or uncertainty. I wanted to ensure peace and joy around the clock on my own little strength, so I was easily frazzled and avoided confrontation at all costs.

Leaving for college was scary, but I always kept a few security blankets nearby to aid in big life changes. Since I still idolized every word my mother said, I rehearsed her mantra frequently: *You have to face your fears in order to be unafraid.* With that reminder, I lived in my freshman dorm with a complete stranger. Yet, my blanket was tied onto two close friends living down the hall. I also reminded myself that my mom was only an hour and a half away from the University of Georgia.

The diversity and distractions of a large SEC school actually appealed to my ingrained social appetite. To give you an accurate picture: the acclaimed comedy show *FRIENDS* came to a close my freshman year, and it was a direct parallel to my life at the time: excessive dependence on friendships and corresponding approval based entirely on situational security. *FACEBOOK* replaced *FRIENDS*, my sophomore year, and the "screen friendship" era via social media took off rapidly after my graduation from UGA. Thankfully, FOMO (fear of missing out) syndrome didn't come into effect until social media really became mainstream long after I had left college life; otherwise, its effects would have hit me hard. Again, I was unknowingly protected through counterbalance. I sort of stepped away from screens in the name of keeping my routine. The new fad felt full of possible stress and confrontation, which didn't fit into my calendar or my control at the time.

꧁꧂

During those new days of making new friends, I was fortunate enough to find a best friend in someone of the opposite sex. My predictable and harmful pattern continued. I shifted my worship of my friends to that of my new boyfriend, while still stressfully trying to balance approval and acceptance from everyone else. Matthew was an idyllic companion for many reasons, and everyone in my inner circle overwhelmingly approved. However, our broken backgrounds allowed us to set each other too high on our proverbial pedestals. We didn't have to carve any wood to easily create idols out of each other. Disappointment was inevitable.

I remember telling Matthew that *I would never ever lie to him, and I expected him to do the same.* Likewise I remember him saying, *I will never ever betray you, and I expect you to do the same.* Matthew and I made little gods out of each other for seven years, growing in love but shrinking in humility. Seven years of dating may seem a little lingered for a couple who didn't meet in high school, nor lived together prior to marriage, but for us, the growth process took extra time. Sadly we were not mature enough to recognize our need for growth in faith, but thanks be to God—He took the reins. We pressure packed our relationship until the eruption affected every aspect of our lives. Thankfully God hid all our band-aids so that we were forced to see how deep our depravity could dwell without His antidote.

Just after our grand proposal at Rockefeller Center in New York City, which corresponded perfectly to our grandiose prideful relationship, I learned that Matthew had been unfaithful to me multiple times throughout our relationship. Even though the fears I dreaded were becoming a reality, my self-righteous pride only increased. Everyone I knew had an "opinion" on the sad situation, and everyone seemed to know what God would have me do, except for me. I spent a lot of time alone that year. I lost confidence, companions, and control, but I gained a new first love: the words of Truth. The Bible became real— not just another story to admire—but oxygen I desperately needed to breathe.

I learned to hear God's voice and lean on Him rather than on another person. I realized that my plans were flawed without His guidance. The Bible wasn't a popsicle to distract me from reality. It was reality, so I saturated myself in it. The words mirrored my sins in a way that was painful at first glance. However, after staring deeply into that mirror, the words against my wounds proved trustworthy and redemptive. Instead of living as a cultural Christian, I was ready to surrender and pursue Christ as the only worthy one to worship despite how that new direction might be perceived by others I loved. I learned to seek God's approval alone, which lightened my stress load; I could not feasibly please everyone anymore. I'd hoped and prayed God would grant me a fresh new relationship so that I could sweep the messy one behind me, but that would not have forced me to face more than one fear simultaneously.

When the news of my fiancé's infidelity was uncovered, my world felt shattered and chaotic. I longed for a fresh start and that included every aspect of my life. I didn't want the same rhythms or routines. I desperately needed to fill my spaces with newness. I was tired of the opinions and assumptions all around me, and I was tired of people treating me like a wounded animal. *Pity can actually produce more pride.* For the first time, I was drawn to new kinds of people, new pastimes, and new personal preferences. Avoiding social interactions was abnormal for me, but I had a lot of "firsts" that year. In order to evade self-pity, I subconsciously **saturated** on all that was true, noble, and lovely. I volunteered for the first time when it was not a requirement. I went on my first mission trip to **serve** at an orphanage. I read my Bible daily and listened to Christian music regularly for the first time. I learned to be **still** and pray without an agenda. Looking back, God had set me in places to strengthen me and **settle** me by stripping off all the sticky, secular band-aids I had carelessly placed on myself. Instead of dealing with my anxiety-ridden circumstances safely and secularly, I started to scrape off the adhesive and clean the wounds.

At the time of my broken engagement, I was working at a brain and spinal cord rehabilitation hospital. My officemate was a paraplegic, and we worked with families who were absorbing medical information about their loved ones with a recent traumatic injury. This job alone was a perfect step in changing my wounded *perspective.* My "hurts" were NOTHING compared to theirs. I also moved back home in order to put myself through graduate school, which gave me a change of scenery and a new focus. Moreover, I met a new friend going through her own relational problems and spiritual growth, which provided me with fellowship. Through all of this, I began to expose the keys to unlock my thought life to battle future anxiety: **saturation, service,** and **stillness.** However, it would take more than one personal crisis to solidify this **settlement.**

After breaking off our first engagement, I'd say the idea that Matthew and I would ever have a healthy or happy life together was akin to standing in front of an ocean with no raft while an army approaches from behind. There is death on all sides: an impossible solution. Facing your darkest fears though, frees you from fragility. Strength of a different spirit, a Holy Spirit, can emerge if you don't hide the pain with a band-aid. God is in the mission of the impossible. He can split an ocean so you can walk right through the middle, and in the process, your fears will drown in a perfect love.

Like the patients I worked with at the rehab hospital, our journey was long and hard, but in the end, Matthew and I did learn how to walk again. In fact we walked through an ocean, and we didn't drown; just our fears did. *"There is no fear in love. But love, perfect love, drives out fear because fear has to do with punishment. The one who fears is not made perfect in love."*[18] Our love was no longer "perfect," but we finally understood a perfect love beyond ourselves. There was no need to place unrealistic expectations on each other to satisfy all our needs or desires because God filled us fully. Rather than going back to a different ocean or a different army, God's perfect love redeemed our relationship through an outright miracle. *"It was good for me to be afflicted so that I might learn your word"*[19]. I did get to start a fresh new relationship with a fresh new person. That person just happened to be the same Matthew with a new, beautifully humble identity. I hoped to emulate this humility, due to the fact that my pride was still as poignant as a powerful wave.

5
Eternal and Extinguished

"I sought the Lord, and he answered me; he
delivered me from all my fears".

— Psalm 34:4

*H*eartache and hard times seem to come like heat: in
waves. We receive a stride of respite and relief to keep us
going. Then, we are crushed and pummeled from wave
upon wave; we gulp for air and hang in the balance for the
next uncertainty.

Once upon a time, I would anxiously pray and wonder
when my time of turmoil would hit next. My fears developed
through protagonist replacement. I'd put myself in someone's
shoes that didn't fit me and anxiously prepare for the same
outcome. But when we prepare for the waves that we see

hitting other people, we miss the present stretches of sand meant for our enjoyment. Waves are unavoidable at some point, but knowing the One who made the oceans, gives us a level of ease no matter our circumstances. When I hear of others hurting, my heart hurts too, but I have hope, and I hope for those hurting, pray for them, and look for ways to **serve** them. We don't have to wonder how we would endure someone else's tragedy. Their wave is not our wave. Their story is not our story, and we have not received the grace and strength needed to endure such a blow.

We should carry burdens together to unify relationships and communities, but we don't have to let the burdens weigh us down. There is a greater peace that surpasses all human comfort, and as the disciple Peter notes, those who suffer will again be restored and actually rejoice in praise because their faith has been refined and proven more genuine than gold.[20] It's not a matter of if, but when hardships will come. Like death, difficulties are inevitable. We just have to see each moment as it relates to our overall story. The ones with twists, turns, and triumphs over evil make for tales worth telling anyway, especially when we persevere toward ending fearlessly.

Besides, there always seems to be subtle ways in which we are prepared for the future: a dream, an accident, or even a clue can come without meaning until after the fact. Much of Jesus' life was a strange enigma to his loved ones until after he ascended to Heaven. *Hindsight will solidify many hypotheses.* Over-preparedness merely justifies our fear of losing control, and pride sits at the root of this justification. We think we know what is best for ourselves because we are the only ones living our lives. Like a stubborn child or ornery adolescent, we do not want someone above us telling us what is best. The "unknown" causes us to tighten our grip on that perceived control. This fear of the unknown pushes many steady people into panic attacks.

We strive to be "overly prepared" in the name of responsibility and good sense, but really we dread being caught off guard. No one is designed to endure constant chaos, which is why control over our surroundings feels safe and favorable; the world was designed with natural patterns and boundaries. Yet, be that as it may, once we live through enough bombshells, we see that our control lies among one simple choice: either keep fighting the wind for power, or fully surrender the fight, freeing ourselves from the anxiety associated with an invisible war: the war for control.

Oswald Chambers once said, "Our natural inclination is to be so precise--trying always to forecast accurately what will happen next--that we look upon uncertainty as a bad thing. We think that we must reach some predetermined goal, but that is not the nature of the spiritual life. The nature of the spiritual life is that we are certain in our uncertainty... when we have the right relationship with God, life is full of spontaneous, joyful uncertainty and expectancy."[21] Thus, if we "raise a white flag" to preparedness, and focus on the simplicity of daily decisions, we will discover that our responsibility remains in what we "absorb," what we allow into our eyes, ears, brain and heart, which will determine the angle of our anxiety.

☙❧

My heart was settled after Matthew and I were married. In fact, the first year of marriage was unexpected bliss. Matthew and I had faced hell and high water prior to our nuptials; we received individual counseling, couples counseling, and ultimately surrendered our lives and our relationship to God (known to be the Wonderful Counselor), trusting He would use it for His glory. He graciously gave us the opportunity to help other couples through their own turmoil, which gave sweet purpose to our previous pains. The reassurance we received after our wedding day coupled with continued rejoicing and respite prepared us for what was ahead.

When I first met Matthew in college, I was also going through unusual health problems as it related to reproductivity. For this reason, Matthew and I decided that after all we'd experienced, the wisest route to take (in any given area of life) was to open our hands completely and trust God with the outcome. In other words, we wrote God a blank check with our lives and future family, and we sought to walk faithfully until He called us home, reminding each other of His constant faithfulness in our past.

Matthew and I were told it would take a while to get pregnant, and even if we conceived a child, we probably would not meet him or her the first several times. To prepare myself for this reality, I subconsciously began to expect the worst from God. Like the disciples on a nearly sinking ship while Jesus napped at the stern, I knew He had the power to save me, but I lacked trust in His goodness. I would quietly cry out to Him, "Don't you care that I'm going to drown?" Nevertheless, God intended for me to *mature in my faith* as a way to prepare me for deeper oceans and harder waves that would eventually lead to my fearless faith.

Despite what medical advice predicted, we were pregnant with our first son after our first year of marriage, and we met Silas on his due date almost two years after our wedding day. Yet again, in His love for me, God gave me some needed prep work when Silas went straight to the neonatal intensive care unit after birth. Because of simple breathing issues, our newborn baby was unexpectedly taken out of my arms and thrust into a world of tubal feedings, alarms, and monitors. If only I could have appreciated the mild nature of this four-day storm compared to what lay ahead.

As with any new parent, there was a whole new bag of potential fears and control issues that came with the prestigious new title. A vast array of choices and routes existed and even more are available for a quick preview due to technological advances today: safe or secular, organic or commercial, public or private, homeopathic or pediatric, the methodological list is inexhaustible and simultaneously exhausting many moms and dads today. The most arduous change involves a person's identity. Even the most sensible and prudent individuals are shaken by an identity crisis at some point after becoming a parent. This identity corresponds with our perception of our place in the world. It is usually subconscious, but substantial all the same.

After having to face open aggression in all directions for my spousal choice, it was easier to make personal choices without caring about how they were perceived by others with regard to my children. However, I still had layers of pride to pull back. I remember how much I struggled with the tension between staying home and educating one little mind with basic communication or returning full-time to the classroom, preparing older minds to deconstruct and analyze various forms of communication. Teaching with paper presented an abundance of opportunities for engagement, while cloth diapers really only presented two opportunities. Thus, my dilemma came down to simple math, which proved I was ready to take on more responsibility outside our home to increase my own engagement.

That's when I was given an opportunity that appeared potentially perfect. I accepted an English teaching position at a local college, which afforded me my days with my son and a few nights a week as Professor Smith. The shiny allure of title tempted my need for validation and identity. Thanks be to God that circumstances beyond my control actually took over postponing my start date and all my prepared syllabi. Looking back at my thoughts during the proposed job offer, God was already preparing my heart to change. I had privately journaled:

> *I believe strongly that I am fulfilling a great purpose in my role as a wife and mother. I know that it's not the countless times I am wiping... wiping snotty noses, wiping watery eyes, wiping dirty bottoms, wiping sandy feet, wiping muddy hands. No.... it's not the wiping that I focus on. I know that I'm nurturing, teaching, building, and investing in life itself. And I truly love it. I know this is both a noble and essential responsibility even if I am becoming a minority in this profession. But*

it's the scary space in between that tears away at my confidence...

Whether it is the guilt of working away from your family, the struggles of working only among your family, or somewhere in between, whatever you do only has value if you are doing it within the perspective of thanksgiving and grace. And if it is a day where you feel your perspective is one that will affect everyone negatively, CHOOSE to change that perspective. After all, the sunrise is new each day, why can't each day be new with it?

What I didn't realize at the time, was that we can't always change our *perspective* on our own strong will or positive self-talk. It is only by the hand of God's grace that we can really change it.

߬Ձ

Just after learning my college course was canceled, I also learned that I was miscarrying a child. God's gracious hand took that tiny life home to heaven just after we had heard his little heartbeat, which made my heart hurt all the more when it happened. More than that, I simultaneously started experiencing debilitating physical pain that doctor's could not diagnose at the time. Rushing to the emergency room gave me a new glimpse of a medical world that I had never known, but would soon become overly acquainted. Still, God's grace filled me with an unexpected joy in ways that I would have otherwise overlooked without the pain. The love from our community after our miscarriage, the love from my toddler, and the hope from my heavenly father was delicately distinct. It was a love that I felt more purely through suffering, and rather than fearing another miscarriage, my pain counterintuitively grew my faith, which increased my hope and ultimate peace. *"Peace I leave with you; my peace I give you. I do not give to you as the world gives. Do not let your hearts be troubled and do not be afraid."*[22] While the deepest pain exists in not getting to meet that precious life, I know it will be Christmas morning when we meet in Heaven one day. The physical pain eventually subsided, and I was strongly encouraged to wait the appropriate amount of time before trying to conceive again.

Instead of trying to control our family's timetable though, we held strong to God's initial conviction for us: we should keep our hands open and trust Him with the outcome until He said otherwise. As God would have it, we were pregnant well before the doctor's recommendation, but as doctors would likely note, there were many "red flags" at the beginning of my third pregnancy. Every time we went for an obstetric appointment, we were certain we had lost another baby, but every time, there was a strong heartbeat. When things finally settled into my second trimester, I was blindsided by another wave of shock.

My water started breaking slowly at twenty-seven weeks gestation, so I was admitted to the hospital for the duration of my pregnancy on strict bedrest. After three days and no signs of distress, it was beyond alarming when doctor's unplugged my hospital bed that was filled with blood and rushed me into an operating room shouting, "We need more nurses in here!" What should have been an episode on a medical drama actually felt like a tranquil dream to me. I was under no medication and had no family with me in the OR, but I had a strange sense of calm surrounding me, which I can only attribute to the Holy Spirit. As nurses and physicians looked panicked and confused, I was given an anesthesia so that they could try and rescue my baby. Levi Joseph Smith came into the world weighing just a little over two pounds. While he may have been anxious to join the world twelve weeks early, he has always exhibited more patience and peace than most adults I've known. The rollercoaster of emotions that surrounded the first few days of Levi's existence would continue through the first few years of his life. The ride was more like a marathon that required callouses: thickened skin that I'd never felt before then. Any work that takes strength, stamina, and long-suffering hurts the most in the beginning before those callouses are formed. I started to feel the rough skin on my fingers, knuckles, feet, and knees, a week after giving birth to little Levi. However, I earnestly prayed that my heart wouldn't callous over during the process. I wanted it to remain soft, malleable, and open like my new micro-preemie's heart.

I remember walking through the halls of Northside Hospital for a few quiet moments as I tried to digest all that had happened 72 hours after his emergency c-section, which I was not conscious to witness. I felt unsure of why so many strangers wanted to help me and my family at that time. I wondered because I didn't think we were experiencing anything more than anyone else. People around the world face unimaginable pain every moment of the day. My troubles didn't seem any more significant. Yet, I realized that this was my first encounter with full-time hospital living. It opened my eyes to a new world that many had already known as "home"—cancer families, traumatic injury families, physically disabled families, and bereavement families. Pain and joy were strangely mixed all over the hospital campus, and loving or helping each other was a natural part of the process. I'd never been less occupied with myself and more interested in others than while visiting Levi for almost 150 days during his NICU occupancy.

2 Corinthians 1:3-5 became another reality I could personally practice: *"Praise be to the God and Father of our Lord Jesus Christ, the Father of compassion and the God of all comfort, who comforts us in all our troubles, so that we can comfort those in any trouble with the comfort we ourselves receive from God. For just as we share abundantly in the sufferings of Christ, so also our comfort abounds through Christ."*

During the first month of Levi's life at Northside, I recall the ups and downs of exhaustion, hormones, and shock. I questioned Levi's very existence. Were we asking this little life to fight, living on machines, when he'd rather rest in peace? Were we wrong to keep him fighting without his consent? When such questions, fears, and emotions swept over me, I'd hear whispers of comfort that I couldn't deny. *"In all this you greatly rejoice, though now you may have had to suffer grief in all kinds of trials. These have come so that your faith may prove genuine".*[23]

Whether it's a child making decisions that break our hearts piece by piece, a spouse who's chosen a road that we believe will break our marriage in half, a parent who we feel like we are having to parent ourselves, or some other relationship that involves us having to stand by and helplessly watch someone we love experience pain that we wished we could erase, we all experience suffering in our own way and in our own time. It truly gives the foundation of faith purpose. Why would anyone want to watch their supposed savior and king suffer on a cross the way that Jesus' followers did? Because He knew we'd all suffer one day, and we needed a way out. I'm thankful that there is purpose in pain.

As I drove home from yet another disappointing visit with Levi that first month, I remembered that I had prayed many times to never be "comfortable or stagnate in my life." I'd found that when things were easy, and I would get too comfortable, I would lose the ability to really hear God's voice, and I would end up trying to take control of the wheel again, which only increased my anxiety. But on that particular day in spring of 2015 I heard him loud and clear: *"You are still going to this hospital because I still have people for you to meet. You don't know the people that will come across your path, but it's not always for you to know. Trust me. Lean on me. I'll carry you when you get tired because I love you, and I love Levi more than you could ever know."*

Once more, God was preparing me for the final wave of shock that would help extinguish my anxiety. I had to choose to trust God when we brought Levi home almost five months after his birth. He had a permanent feeding tube, an oxygen tank, a heart monitor, a laundry list of medicines, and an appointment-packed schedule with doctors and therapists indefinitely. The finish line for this new marathon was nowhere in sight. I couldn't rush this season even if I wanted to callous up and sprint. I had to settle in for the long haul, but this also kept me from wasting the season. Abolishing anxiety would only come (for my prideful, prepared, and particular self) through fully surrendering again and again and again. Then *abiding* would more naturally occur. I needed to see the world through multiple lenses in order to gain a kingdom, rather than worldly, *perspective*. Little did I know, I would receive a hard "heavenly perspective" just a month after Levi came home.

6

Sleeplessness and Senses

"Many things — such as loving, going to sleep, or behaving unaffectedly — are done worst when we try hardest to do them."

— C.S. Lewis

I felt like I was gripping the side of a skyscraper balcony hanging on for dear life and each time someone or something tried to touch a single finger, I screamed. My exhaustion and fear had blended to create a sort of anger that felt displaced. I didn't know why I was angry, but with every two-year old tantrum, monitor mis-alarm, potty accident, or tangled medical cord, I snapped with frustration. There was really no reason to be angry, which made it all worse. I didn't have a person to blame, but I yielded to the fear and exhaustion. It was all related to fear. Fear I'd never get more than a wink of shut eye again. Fear that someone or something else would raise my sons because I couldn't find the time. I was afraid I wouldn't maintain any priorities: no time to spend with God, no time to spend with my husband, no time to be the creative and devoted mother and wife I wanted to be. I was afraid I'd spend all my time *doing* rather than *being*. How could I regain the peaceful *perspective* that I'd held in the hospital? I didn't think there was anyone who could fix my fears because I didn't want others living with us or taking my children away just so I could learn to sit still again. I wanted to be the super mom I had heard about in books and articles. I wanted to be able to show peace and patience that only comes from God's presence. So I would sit still, praying for wisdom to take the next step. Those steps, though, had to be *intentional*. Not only was I a new parent of two little boys under two, but one of them currently suffered from medical fragility and a notebook of possible future disabilities. The only thing that was steady in my life, besides my marriage, was my conversations with God and His word, which continued to increase in palatability. God answered my prayers for *perspective*, and while many hard roads continued, they became easier to handle after my previous victories.

I recalled a story I had heard about a man who had been sitting at a red light for what seemed like days. He was inching his way to the traffic light at snail speed trying to maintain his composure as he was already extremely late for a very important meeting. Finally, he only had one car in front of him. Suddenly the woman chose to get out of her car and rummage through the back seat. She was certainly trying to move quickly, but he couldn't believe that she chose that moment to grab something from the back. The light turned green, and she continued to scurry around in the back. He laid on the horn to give her a reminder of their current traffic situation, but she didn't budge. More cars began laying on loud honks as the woman was now holding everyone hostage at this horrific light. Finally, someone heard her scream for help beneath all the honking and ran to her aid. Lo and behold, the woman had an infant who was choking in her back seat. While the story has multiple morals, it reminded me that we don't always know the full picture of our current state, even when we think we do.

There may be many reasons why God gave us the children that he did, or the ones that he didn't, but it's not always clear at the first or second traffic jam. We assume through compare and contrast conversations that the situation is clear when spiritual reality knows a third mode of explanation. Without trusting in an unknown God for that which we can't prove, we put ourselves back in God's role, thereby increasing our anxiety. Providence proves God's handiwork in every tiny detail of our lives, freeing us from trying to know all those details ahead of time.

When little Levi was living in the intensive care unit, I realized that his amazing medical team was only treating him with the information and details they had on hand. Doctors were always, in effect, "Practicing medicine." Without new research and new discoveries, they didn't always know what or how to treat their new patient. They must observe their surroundings, utilize their past expertise, and make an informed decision, but those decisions can change from day to day. The same is true with every job; we forget to challenge our own experiences with humility and the right questions. Levi's birth gave me a new *perspective* on what I thought I knew as a parent, a wife, and even a human being.

∞×∞

Levi was a constant "spitter." He had multiple surgeries before coming home with us and afterwards, but one in particular was intended to keep him from vomiting. Sadly it was a wasted procedure because Levi learned to bypass that knot tied in his stomach almost immediately; to this day, he has the strongest gag reflex of anyone I know. Levi's gastric doctor was never happy with his weight gain on the national growth chart. I never had to fear him choking at a traffic light, though, because he threw up everything we put in his feeding tube for the first year of his life, literally. We kept buckets around our house and in our car for his purging purposes. Personally, I'm surprised we didn't cause more traffic jams trying to catch the amount of liquid expelling from the poor baby at any given moment. His big brother, Silas, even learned how to manage chaotic intestinal messes at his young age because he was my constant care companion. This predicament was ironic, being that one of my strongest childhood anxieties involved the fear of throwing up outside the privacy and comfort of my home.

Most people didn't know what to think of Levi when he was an infant, let alone help take care of him. I once tried to check on Levi as he made choking sounds in the car, and I realized I veered a bit in the other lane. I received a death stare from the car that later came up next to me. And later that same day, while I was in a store, everyone looked at my baby boy with pathetic eyes because his legs were casted from his diaper to his toes. One man asked if his legs were wrapped so that he didn't hurt himself. I wasn't quite sure what he meant, but either way, it was clear that no one really knew how NOT to glare or stare at us.

୫୦୦ଓ

There was one person besides his medical team that immediately knew how to love on Levi. My best friend, godly mentor, and sister in Christ, Kyra Karr, was a missionary in Rome when Matthew and I married, and we were able to stay with her and her husband, Reid, on our honeymoon. Because they only came home every couple of years, it was a miracle that her third daughter and my first son were born around the same time during her first sabbatical. Then, God orchestrated her second stateside visit during the birth of little Levi.

Levi and Kyra bonded the first time they met. She was unafraid of his wires, his casts, or his cumbersome state; she wasn't scared to try to help with his feeding therapy even if he choked and gaged in the process, and she didn't mind swaying his heavy casted body until he conked out in her arms. She had three daughters of her own, all born healthy and full-term, but she looked at Levi as if he was the most beautiful baby she'd ever seen.

Kyra was never from this world. She always belonged in Heaven. She was my dearest friend, and she went to be with her Creator and Savior the exact day, one year after my unborn baby went to Heaven. As an amazing sister, mother, daughter, wife, and friend, that baby couldn't be in better arms. They are united with many who are living in eternal peace, joy and love. I feel sad for those who never had the chance to know her light and contagious joy, but I thank God every day that I got to spend those special moments with her just days before she left this Earth. While nothing seemed to make sense right after I found out about her death, I can look back at God's grace that she came and lived my life with me the summer Levi finally came home. She took care of my boys and myself like we were her flesh and blood, and I think she did that for everyone she knew.

While it's easy to idolize someone who is no longer living and making mistakes, Kyra did have a rare wisdom that many don't attain until all their hair is gray. I don't know how Silas (two years-old at the time) could have known how she passed away, but after hearing that Kyra was in Heaven, Silas said, "She is not in her red truck anymore." We never mentioned the horrific collision she and her family had with a fully loaded semi truck, so I don't know how he knew except that it was the Holy Spirit speaking through my son. He then said, "And Levi will not have his 'shoes' in Heaven," (his shoes were what Silas called his casts) to which I responded, "Yes, we will all have new perfect heavenly bodies with no casts!" Silas then said that he wanted to bring Kyra's little girls a band-aid, a hug, and some applesauce to make them feel better. The simplicity of a child's heart provides the starting point for our own healing in trauma.

I do not know the horrors of unexpectedly losing a grown child, but I know Kyra's family, as well as my own, can attest to the grace and peace that pervades painful circumstances.

Those waves of shock shake you to pursue a new way of living; one that banishes anxiety and replaces it with power. Kyra's husband, Reid, explained the transformative power of Christ's grace better than me for those who lean on Him in fear and tragedy:

> "A new life in Christ is radically different than the previous one, in which we were enslaved to fear, worry, uncertainty, and sin. Faith in Christ frees the believer and radically transforms his *perspective* on life. The fear, worry, and uncertainty of the old life is replaced by peace, hope, and the certainty of salvation. By no means, however, does faith in Christ guarantee a life free of hardship and suffering. It is, in fact, the opposite. Suffering is not an exception for the believer, but the norm. The apostle Paul warns his disciple that all who desire to live a godly life in Christ will experience suffering (2 Timothy 3:12). Trials are to be expected. **The hope of the gospel, however, is that life in Christ frees us from the fear that suffering and trials produce. Whereas sin enslaves us to fear, the gospel frees us from fear and enslaves us to grace** [emphasis added]. The apostle states clearly, 'After you have suffered a little while, the God of all grace, who has called you to his eternal glory in Christ, will himself restore, confirm, strengthen, and establish you.'" (1 Peter 5:10).[24]

For a missionary man raising three daughters alone, this *perspective* seems unreal, yet I can personally affirm it's seemingly unnatural because the Spirit of God is "supernatural." He is the One who gives us the power to feel peace and hope in trauma, nothing and no one else can do that. It is much like having a baby or raising a child. It's incredibly painful, it's disturbingly daunting, and the potential perils fill the heart and mind from start to finish. Still, the joy that pervades this "unnatural" process has kept humans down the path of parenting since the beginning of time.

What then is to be said when we cannot feel God's Spirit? When the pain or fear is so great that we have no words to pray, let alone gain *perspective*? There are words written for those very times:

> "He has made me chew on gravel.
> He has rolled me in the dust.
> Peace has been stripped away,
> and I have forgotten what prosperity is.
> I cry out, "My splendor is gone!
> Everything I had hoped for from the Lord is lost!"
> The thought of my suffering and homelessness
> is bitter beyond words.
> I will never forget this awful time,
> as I grieve over my loss.
> Yet I still dare to hope
> when I remember this:
> The faithful love of the Lord never ends!
> His mercies never cease.
> Great is his faithfulness;

his mercies begin afresh each morning.
I say to myself, "The Lord is my inheritance;
therefore, I will hope in him!"
The Lord is good to those who depend on him,
to those who search for him.
So it is good to wait quietly for salvation from the
Lord".[25]

In other words, we cry out, we grieve, and we wait because we choose to trust in the unknown until it is made known, just like a child must wait on a regular basis. They cry, grieve, and wait (usually impatiently) until their mom or dad reassures them with words that change their *perspective* or until their circumstances change altogether. Note the emphasis on obtaining God's mercy, or unmerited favor, EVERY morning. We do not have to be anxious about tomorrow or how we will deal with the next week or month or year of our life because God's good graces are sufficient for each day—and not needed ahead of time.

If I trusted in the God who gave me miraculous children when I was told I couldn't, and a miraculous marriage when I was told I shouldn't, how could I now say that I wouldn't trust God who took away a miraculous woman from a husband and daughters who "needed" her most of all? Knowing that a thirty year-old mom of three girls was not "needed" in this world provided me with a great pride leveler. Even my little fragile Levi would make it just fine in the world without me. *I finally reconciled the paradox of pride:* I was infinitely and eternally loved and chosen by God to be His daughter and to be an integral part of His plans, yet I was a non-essential part of the grand scheme of life. I am a gift, but just like gifts, I am not a need. I am a temporary joy just as my family is to me, and I get to be a part of God's family and His plans rather than the other way around. Moreover, *facing the fragility of life aided in the abolishment of my anxiety.* "I know that everything God does will endure forever; nothing can be added to it, and nothing taken from it. God does it so that people will *fear Him.*"[26] Now I had a new kind of "fear" to understand. If life was such a breath and each moment such a gift, I wanted to savor it all by seeking the Lord constantly, and learning contrition of heart in order to fear nothing but Him. However, the lack of sleep, physical exhaustion, and increased illnesses I endured over the first five years of Levi's life were seeking to steal my joy and *perspective.*

∞∞∞

Matthew and I were strongly advised by doctors NOT to get pregnant after Levi's birth for at least eighteen months, preferably his second birthday, which would give my body time to heal from traumatic surgery in hopes that I could carry another baby longer. The intense warning came from unknowns about my body and what could potentially happen to me if I were carrying a child too soon. There were hints at illness and even death for both the baby and myself. This put fear into the heart of my strong husband. He had already lost a brother, a baby, and now watched me lose a best friend, he couldn't discuss losing his wife that soon too. Despite all of this, though, we felt we needed to pray fervently and ask God to make it clear how we would fear only Him in this decision.

That said, we faithfully sought His will as we had done before we had any children. We tried to reconcile doctor's orders with God's directive. As He would have it, we were not "trying" to have another baby when we found out at Levi's first birthday that we were pregnant again.

We still had a few "scares" to undergo during this fourth pregnancy, but overall our third baby boy seemed to grow beautifully until doctors requested an early c-section for precautionary measures. Sometimes soldiers are deployed to the same awful location whether they like it or not, but they carry a badge of honor for their calling. While I may not have wanted a third deployment to the neonatal intensive care unit, that was my calling for a time, and it actually felt like an honor. We already had the supplies, training, and tactics in place since Levi had just left the hospital sixteen months prior to Roman's arrival. Like a NICU veteran, Roman Samuel was born on Veteran's Day and helped strengthen his big brother, Levi, in more ways than one. What's more, I was now learning to lace up my own bootstraps like a vet or in my case, a nurse, because every single sleep cycle I enjoyed was disrupted for several years after Roman's birth.

All of my boys began to pass around common illnesses, which is a typical component of having little kids, but it felt more debilitating in my case due to Levi's strictly scrutinized weight gain. No one wants to eat when he is ill, so we teetered on trying to get Levi to eat by mouth and simply succumbing to a lifetime of tubal supplements since he was always sick. "Pandemic mask-wearing" was not yet a part of culture, and I didn't want to shelter my kids in one place just to avoid germs, thereby recreating hypochondriac fears from my own childhood. As such, I embraced and expected a lack of good health in all our lives for the foreseeable future, forgetting some of God's goodness in the process.

I remember Kyra once telling me, after having her three babies and a constant barrage of sickness, "If we are called to take our thoughts captive, then we should do the same with our emotions or hormones." Our feelings/hormones or what I will call our "senses," should not rule over us any more than our thoughts and anxiety should. Although, our thought-life sets the stage for dispelling anxiety, a lack of sleep or health problems make the command to "take your thoughts captive and make them obedient to Christ"[27] feel somewhat unattainable. It is the "new mercies" every day that we must trust when we don't "feel" anything new in our own circumstances.

Kyra's advice was invaluable wisdom when I found out I would give birth a fourth time in five years. Fear could have wreaked havoc on me, as well as my pregnancy hormones, but I kept hearing, *"Do not fear, for I am with you; do not be dismayed, for I am your God. I will strengthen you and help you; I will uphold you with my righteous right hand."*[28] Succumbing to our senses is an easy scapegoat with a lousy gain. We lose *perspective* when we let hormones dictate our direction. On the other hand, dissecting how we "feel" in any given moment proves that our thoughts and emotions cannot be trusted, nor should they stake claim on our future choices. We have a personal decision: submit to the emotions of the moment, or have our emotions submit to the one who created them.

Having a best friend live in a different culture gave me a fresh *perspective* on my own senses and circumstances, because culture can influence or incorrectly validate how we feel in any given moment. With Kyra gone, though, I had to stand on my own story without her advice or missional guidance.

৪෩

The word "mission" has multiple definitions, including humanitarian work, faith-based service, and the act of being specifically sent. In all its meanings, I was not a missionary, and I did not take part in any mission work until I was in my twenties. It was then that I saw a variety of needs in Haiti, Ecuador, Spain, and the United States. One thing all these trips had in common was the element of discomfort. Whether physical, emotional, or otherwise, attending a mission trip never looks similar to our daily life. It is an experience that erases our normal routine for the sake of serving others. When we are forced to cease all habitual activity, it's akin to having a bedridden illness without the remote or medication. We freeze our life, and see others through a different lens, a new *perspective.* Observing divergent cultures builds an awareness of our ability to rationalize "wants" as "needs," but when life becomes comfortable again, our tolerance level decreases and our "needs" increase.

Mission trips, as well as hospital stays, have stripped me of what I thought I needed to thrive. I had always been an eight-hour-a-night sleeper, and a task-orientated, productive individual. But with four boys under five, I was laid bare without sleep, without good food, without checking anything off my "to-do" list, and usually without friends, family, or what America would call "fun." Yet, I had an abundance of community **saturating** me in God's word, a sweet measure of purposeful **stillness**, and a kind of **service** like I had never known. After our fourth son, Luca, was born without a NICU stay, we were shocked when he was later sent from the emergency room to the PICU (pediatric intensive care unit) at three months of age. God was stripping me from a "need" pattern, to a fearless faith pattern.

Little Luca B. was diagnosed with a subglottic hemangioma at three months-old. Basically he was born with a large blood clot or birthmark covering half of his airway. Instead of breathing through a hose, Luca was born breathing through a straw. His illness created many sleepless nights because his other brothers happened to be simultaneously screaming in the night due to their own undiagnosed illnesses and weight loss. Right after Levi was given the approval to extract his feeding tube and eat solely by mouth, Roman started losing weight and wouldn't eat much of anything the entire second year of his life. At the same time, I was trying to help my newborn medicate in order to obtain oxygen. Shortly before all of this, God had again given me preparation for my hospital frequencies through a vivid dream…

೭౦ా

I awoke from the dream completely exhausted by the realistic nature of my imaginary turmoil. I had left Luca in some sort of nursery while attending a friend's big event. Because I was unavoidably detained longer than the nursery hours, I assumed my other friends would retrieve my sweet baby and bring him back to me. To my dismay, no one had little Luca.

As I inquired to his whereabouts, I learned he was transferred all over other cities to different nurseries. In a panic, I began to follow his trail. I rode subways, buses, and ran through streets eagerly trying not to fall apart, but every time I had a glimpse of hope, it was shattered. Like many dreams the details are foggy and seemingly ridiculous, but I can say that there were dropped calls, language barriers, and every other formidable obstacle keeping me from my son. Panic set into my bones. I was at an utter loss. The trail ended, and I was sobbing hysterically. Then, as the subway doors opened to the end of the line, there was my husband. He was standing with a general air of normalcy, smiling with Luca in his arms and our other three boys at his sides. None of them had any concern or care in the world. It was as if we were supposed to meet at the subway stop the whole time. My sadness began to melt one happy tear at a time, and I almost felt foolish. That's when I woke up to reality.

The dream may have been a precursor to putting Luca in the ICU for the first time when they couldn't figure out his breathing issues, but I think it might have been a little broader than that. Even though God strengthens me, He also always humbles me so that pride doesn't hinder my *perspective*. Pride is the root of everyone's struggle with sin and separation from an idyllic Eden. It is the lesson we must relearn whether we realize it or not: we do not have to do life alone. Even without biological family nearby, or consistent help available, other people always step into my life and my story exactly when I need them.

We are never alone in this world. God provides beautiful hands to carry our burdens, our kids, our hurts and our joys with us. If we drop our load at any point in time, someone else will surely pick it up, even without our request. That is the humble grace we enjoy in life if we just learn to let go and trust. Then, there is a gratitude that enables us to **serve** and carry other falling loads that we see in the future. It can be easy to take all the credit when people look at my "stair-step" load of kids and praise me for having the "energy" to handle a pack of rowdy boys. However, everyone knows that it takes a village to raise a child. If we let pride convince us that we can handle our load alone, we'll soon forget the humble stance of **stillness** and break down from exhaustion.

For at least two years straight one or more of my children woke me up every single night, literally, and this came after five years of newborn sleep deprivation. Sometimes it felt like a comical joke, and other times my prison sentence. I literally could not predict why or how all my children couldn't simultaneously sleep through the night for seven years. Looking back, I actually adapted a new healthy posture of **saturation** and **stillness** that wouldn't have come any other way. I was always a routine and tightly efficient woman, but I didn't have the energy or desire to hold on to my personal habits anymore. I couldn't exercise on any schedule; I couldn't eat on any schedule; I couldn't have any expectations for my day whatsoever. It was fine to have a very lightly penciled organized agenda, but I **settled** into a more amicable response when those plans dissipated by 8:00 am. While there were very difficult days that forced me into grabbing quick REM sleep at a nearby hotel, (not a joke, my husband forced me to leave the premises for the sake of my sanity more than once) what I gained from my madness was a sense of freedom. I finally took Matthew 11:28-29 literally: *"Come to me, all you who are weary and burdened, and I will give you rest. Take my yoke upon you and learn from me, for I am gentle and humble in heart, and you will find rest for your souls."*

Instead of trying to find a solution to my temporary problem of sleeplessness that felt eternal, I just woke up even earlier and spent more time throughout my day **saturating** in truth and praying in desperation for the strength and endurance to live and love well through my exhaustion. *"I rise before dawn and cry for help; I have put my hope in your word".*[29] Instead of securing a solution to perfect health, I relied on *perspective* to see those whose health was far worse than my own family's. This *perspective* awarded me freedom. My freedom gave way to another level of power that could not have come from my own strength. *"For the Spirit God gave us does not make you timid, but gives you power, love and self-discipline."*[30] Seeking to be **still** before God and let Him lead my day actually showed me how strong He could be through my weaknesses. I witnessed miracles of energy that should not have otherwise been in existence because I wasn't depending on myself anymore, but on God. Note the third gift in the above verse though: *self-discipline*. We may think love and power are great gifts that are easily received, but *self-discipline* means we are having to make some specific choices every moment of the day. God changed me, but I had to change my habits. We can rely on God's promises, but practical steps must be taken in response to those mercies in order to maintain that godly *perspective*, which eradicates anxiety.

7

Good Kind of Busy

"It is not enough to be busy. So are the ants. The question is: What are we busy about?"

— Henry David Thoreau

Wow you're busy!
You got your hands full!
Do you ever rest!?
Looks like you never slow down!
I'm tired just looking at you!
You sure are busy!

There is a natural state of "work" that men and women were designed to perform. According to Harvard Medical School, "A 2016 study of about 3,000 people, published in the *Journal of Epidemiology and Community Health*, suggested that working even one more year beyond retirement age was associated with a 9% to 11% lower risk of dying during the 18-year study period, regardless of health. A 2015 study of 83,000 older adults over 15 years, published in the CDC journal *Preventing Chronic Disease*, suggested that, compared with people who retired, people who worked past age 65 were about three times more likely to report being in good health and about half as likely to have serious health problems, such as cancer or heart disease."[31] Most people can attest to these statistics by their need to feel purposeful. When we watch someone lose their ability to care for themselves, let alone someone else, deterioration sets into their bones at a rapid pace.

However, current technological advances have made it so people do not need to stay busy with mundane tasks that once took so much time. We don't have to make a fire to cook food; we don't have to hang laundry outside to dry; we don't even have to vacuum if we choose to purchase a small robot. But instead of feeling peaceful with more time to rest, read, or relieve others of their burdens, we fill our calendar fuller because we have open space, a void, or time, which our bones tell us need to be filled with more work. Thus, we look for ways to be "busy" so that when someone asks, "how are you?" We can answer, "busy" like everyone else. Sadly, it is not a "good kind of busy" that we are pursuing.

The Bible speaks directly into the importance of women staying busy in their own homes with their own lives lest they "become idle, going from house to house as gossip, busybodies."[32] Moreover, we are all called to *ambitiously* "lead a quiet life: we should mind our own business and work with our hands"[33] Thankfully, I'm not wired for a life of idleness; nonetheless, it's important that I find the right kind of busy regardless of my natural inclination. Everyone has his/her own cross to bear and journey to take, but the natural desire to prepare or compare "busyness" often steals the joy of living in the messy, monotonous moments. We can't just hope to stumble into significant time management, we must <u>choose</u> to be purposeful with our pace. *Otherwise we live in a new oxymoronic, agitated state of "idle busyness."*

I providentially landed on words I wrote for a women's retreat, which centered on the theme of "rest" in a busy culture:

> *We think our significance comes from what we do, not who we are... we feel an unstated need to prove ourselves to ourselves and others by doing rather than being, which makes us weary from working. After understanding insights around the agricultural revolution and juxtaposing those with my own findings in Exodus, I'm convinced we don't have enough people to feed around our large American farm tables. Once upon a time man ate what he had for the day; until learning to "store" our goods, we were not a slave to them. There wasn't "efficiency" in work, there was just "a days work". Now we keep busy running for a future break that may never come.*

As much as I love leftovers, I also see the commonalities between excess in food and excess in cultural life. The more we have, the more we think we need, and the less we trust we will obtain our "daily bread," whatever that may involve. The more efficient we have become as a society, the more time we have. Yet somehow people have managed to use that extra time poorly because so many people describe their lives as "busy" or "stressed." We are filling our bellies fuller than needed and filling our calendars tighter than possible. Why?

Pride keeps us cramming our calendars so that our modern innovations, which have given us more time, don't make us look useless or lazy (unless you've chosen the other extreme and lead a "busy-body" life filled with vanity and vexation). Unfortunately, less physical labor from wonderful inventions has actually created a society with more emotional discomfort. We fear silence because we have an invisible robotic program constantly managing our home, our family, and our wallet. We keep sounds playing around the clock to fill the "dead space." I'm certainly not living in a third world country myself; my own children think it's funny to chat with *Siri*, but I'll admit *my fear exists in submitting to a life of comfort and control and becoming "idly busy" in the process.*

ജാൽ

Since my faith journey had taught me that God's plans were better than mine, and I had little to no control over any area of my life, I wanted to understand what actual choices I had to make to maintain my peaceful *perspective*. Based on university research, various internet sources agree that a person makes around 35,000 choices a day. Between scratching an itch, hitting snooze, or buying a house, every little movement is a choice. How, then, could I make choices that kept me close to my Savior who had saved me so many times so that I stayed far from fear? Nothing else I'd sought had given me peace in chaos like the posture of humility toward God. "Fearing" or revering Him and recognizing His perfect love had changed everything in my life. Couple this with my home/hospital reflection time, and three practical actions had subconsciously been put into practice during my hardest seasons changing my mindset drastically. I established three things I could do to avoid future anxiety in a stressful world: **saturation, service,** and **stillness**—the keys to abiding (remaining) in God's perfect arms at all times, in order to maintain a right *perspective* in all circumstances—peace in brokenness. These keys, along with personal trials, are the *antidote to anxiety*.

Saturation—what we absorb throughout the day: what we read, watch, listen to, scroll through, and the like; that which affects our thought patterns.

Service—what we do throughout the day: how we help others and take the focus off of ourselves; how we view our circumstances and surroundings in light of other people.

Stillness—what we do to be silent: prayer and meditation time or an equivalent humble posture; time to listen rather than speak; recognizing we can't achieve all we set out to achieve on our own; letting go of the reins.

All three added together equal—**Settled**—the absence of a restless heart or restless mind, which leads to unnecessary anxiety; being at peace no matter our position.

Let me break these down.

ꙮ

SATURATION-

Most people watch what they put into their mouths because it affects how they feel physically. Sadly many people don't recognize the direct correlation between what they put into their eyes and ears, which affects how they feel mentally and emotionally. I recently finished a book called, *Competing Spectacles*, that refocused my vision. Doesn't every individual and corporation do the same thing from time to time? Hire a marketing, design, or investment firm, to help us revamp, refresh, or rebrand in order to avoid a total shut down. Partial shut-downs help us find where the paint is chipping or the chips are getting stale, but a full-blown melt down will cripple a company. Closing the doors for a day keeps the collapse away.

Whether it's a revival or a corporate fast, the goal is to remain running, and we need to regain focus and momentum to do that. If not, a slow fade like the end of a broadway spectacle begins to dim our lights; our initial zeal for a cause, a calling, or a company cannot withstand the pitfalls of time. Disenchantment sets in as time progresses. In the same way that time can heal, time can also hurt us when it comes to our self-awareness and resolve. Plus, what better way to distract us from our focus than to have a screen **saturate** our attention every second of the day.

The author of *Competing Spectacles*, Tony Reinke, states, «We are now more media obese than we are physically obese. And we are not happier. We are lonelier. We are more depressed"[34]. Additionally, we are not even aware of our depression or our physique because we continue to consume and binge watch in order to avoid the problem, just as an overweight individual continues eating to avoid facing their weight issue. When culture says something is "normal," then time allows us to relax the initial shock and become anesthetized to it, and then our consumption slowly increases. I'm not saying that everyone who watches *Netflix* is media obese, nor is it wrong to enjoy the luxuries of technology (I certainly appreciate ordering groceries from my phone and having them delivered to my car in the rain). Reinke echoes this notion as well: "The antinomian who watches whatever he wants in the name of Christian freedom is just as naive as the legalist who celebrates his rejection of all television and movies and screen time as evidence of his Christian holiness" (135). A wise person avoids both extremes in humility and wisdom.

While screen time is all relative, when it entered American homes in the 1940s, it changed the world in a greater way than almost any other invention with the exception of transportation. No one is surprised by societal pendulum-swings. Just as we needed more gyms and personal trainers when cars took away our regular cardio activity, we now need to find ways to unplug in order to keep the new obesity of anxiety from rising to national crisis levels. Technology is always a blessing and a curse, but there is a significant difference between a beneficial tool and a bewildering trick. A 2020 documentary entitled *The Social Dilemma* highlights the dangers of tricky technology that **saturates** the human psyche. Former *Google* design ethicist and documentary star, Tristan Harris, explains the difference between the invention of the bicycle and the that of social media or "smart" phones. He says, "A tool [like the bicycle] sits and waits patiently, but if it's not a tool, it demands something from us. We have moved away from technology as a tool and moved towards technology as a manipulation and addiction based environment."[35] Harris further explains that the systems we have created, which we once controlled, are now controlling us because we don't have the same limits and protections in place for our minds or our children's minds that we once had with early television programming.

When Saturday morning cartoons were first created, they strictly limited advertising and aligned restrictions for the safety of our kids. Those initial boundaries have decreased or disappeared all together as time has passed. "When we feel alone, *anxious*, or scared, we have a digital pacifier to assuage us" (Harris, *The Social Dilemma*). At some point we need to take the pacifier away and learn to recognize how to feed our minds healthy nourishment. American mathematician and data scientist, Cathy O'Neil, who is also featured in the film, agrees that the creation of artificial intelligence has erased our understanding of reality and *emotional stability:* "A.I. doesn't know what truth is. It doesn't have a proxy for truth that is better than a click. If we can't agree on what is true, then we can't agree on any of our problems."[36]

Clearly humanity perceives a problem with our injected visual media outlets, but our desire to change that which becomes comfortable and convenient is impossible without great conviction. We need purposeful alterations to our lifestyle akin to ripping off those aforementioned band-aids. When we know there's an infection deeper than the surface, but do nothing to heal it, we risk losing control of ourselves altogether.

For most of my life, I didn't really think about what I was feeding my mind. I filled it with an assorted buffet of ideas, hoping to be well-rounded in the process while simultaneously disregarding the invisible battle that existed in the world. A battle that wages war in our minds. Jesus says, "If you hold to my word, you are really my disciples. Then you will know the truth, and the truth will set you free."[37] *Truth equals freedom.* Moreover, the Lord "sent out his word and healed them; he rescued them from the pit of destruction."[38] Once I felt the dark pit of despair after losing my first fiancé, I began to fill my mind with Truth because I felt I had lived a lie. Without making a conscious decision, I began listening, watching, reading, and taking in mediums that were **saturated** with God's truth, and it literally set me free from fearful thinking. But, let me be clear, I don't believe secular television, mainstream media, or blockbuster cinemas stem from Satan, nor do I presume to avoid all that is not Christian at its core. How would anyone spread Truth if the world were segregated by beliefs? This contradicts Christ's life completely.

Jesus spent a lot of time with the scum of his society despite onlookers' disapproval. He came to save the sick and the broken. However, the majority of his quality time was spent with twelve disciples whom he considered "friends." Jesus knew how to live in the world without being **saturated** by it. Likewise, the amount of time we spend filling our thoughts with farces or fluff like social screening, temporal news stories, marketed material, and the like, will have devastating side effects without any boundaries in place. Our time spent on secular **saturation** should be <u>significantly less</u> than the time we spend absorbing what is pure, right, noble, lovely, admirable, true, excellent, or praiseworthy[39]. If we feed ourselves more junk food than healthy food, it doesn't matter how much exercise we get, we are still hindering our overall internal health.

More than that, there are situations when we may need to completely remove all forms of education and entertainment that pull us down. Rather than simply lessening their quantity, we need to erase their impactful quality. Author Joyce Myer wrote extensively about the, *Battlefield of the Mind,* and our propensity to become lazy with how we **saturate** it: "I think the flesh is lazy and people want to get something from nothing (with no effort on their part); however, that really is not the way [life] works."[40] This explains why "diet fads" came on the scene many years ago. They are a quick fix. Get something without doing anything. In the same way that addicts can't cope in certain environments until they have worked hard to gain freedom and footing in a new environment, mainstream media addicts may also need to step away for a time until they have a new lense for straining out lies and only absorbing truth. "More than anything guard and protect your mind, for life flows from it."[41]

∞

SERVICE-

Clearly mainstream media would acquiesce to the brokenness that exists in the world, which also provides the surfeit of philanthropic opportunities at hand today. We don't have to look hard to find ways to **serve.** Whether it's simply helping our spouse in a hard season, caring for an elderly parent, making food for someone grieving, performing small acts of kindness or large volunteer positions, opportunities to meet someone else's needs are readily available. God promises to meet all our needs anyway, so why not be a part of the process in a way that alters our *perspective* from complaining to caring. Looking for ways to support others will beautifully take care of our needs in the process. There is no time for anxiousness when our perspective shifts to **serving** those most vulnerable around us.

I am far from cynical, but I believe humans are born already knowing how to look after their own interests. Pride and sin don't need to be taught. Even when we teach our children that it is better to give/serve than to receive, for some reason we display those acts of service in isolated moments to people we may never see again. Holidays mark the most popular times to give or **serve,** but real sacrifice and service requires laying down our lives every single day. Family needs are always available but the hardest to selflessly satisfy because this kind of selflessness tends to waver in it's motivation. Why do people continue to give up their needs, wants, desires, rights, or dreams, for others when they never feel as though others are giving equally to them?

Honestly, I don't think people can really be selflessly sacrificial. I think it takes a supernatural love to die to ourselves like that every day. If we know Jesus at all though, we see a life that exists purely for the sake of others. He had no ulterior motive except love. When our desire is to become more like him, He enables us to check our motivations daily and continue to fight against our own selfishness. Our pride tells us that we've done enough. It's our turn to have what we want. We have **served** others so much that we "deserve" a break. Unfortunately, society echoes this chant, making a life mimicking Christ that much more difficult to pursue.

Perfect selflessness does not exist in this life, but that doesn't mean we should stop "taking up our cross" and pursuing the attempt. We should strive to be led by the Spirit and give up our time, our schedule, and our plan, in order to truly find joy in **serving**; only then does our walk look like joy rather than begrudging frustration or self-righteous angst. If a person has never met Jesus though, this feat is impossible, and he/she will only end up serving him/herself and showing everyone around how to do the same. Love requires sacrifice, but God's love required the ultimate sacrifice, which in turn gives us life abundantly.

Instead of seeing our current climate as a monotonous routine, albeit heavy and hard or peaceful and perfect, we choose to see the significance in our ability to care for others in the midst of any season— simply **serve**. Personally, I have been able to meet new faces at doctors offices, emergency rooms, and therapy clinics throughout my journey in motherhood, which I thank God for every day because it reminds me that someone out there is going through a life harder than mine. A season of medical ministry did my soul some good. On the other hand, without proper balance in service, we'll give and sacrifice for a time, and then begin to resent those who are not giving back. When we serve with the expectation of being served in return, we are often bitter and empty.

After having four children in five years, the amount of time spent meeting the needs of other little people all but consumed my life. Without the proper **saturation** and quiet **stillness** to counterbalance it, I would have been a far worse person than before having kids. After my first child was born, I still sought to regain my independence and my identity through busy work, part-time jobs, and a rigid schedule for personal enrichment. All the while subconsciously resenting anyone who didn't have to alter their life or work hard to balance their busyness as I did. Ironically, I couldn't see how deeply rooted my self-serving tendencies were until having a child with a permanent feeding tube and medical fragility.

The more chaotic my life began to look from the outside, the more God transformed my inward tendencies to slow down, sit **still**, and **serve** out of an abundance of gratitude for each new day. Busily caring for my boys and my husband gave me purpose, but God gave me back my identity in Him. He proved that He'd give me time for myself, I just had to ask and say thank you when it came. I couldn't be a martyr, nor could I be a super hero. I could only open my hands and ask for the strength needed for the day ahead. With too much time to serve myself, my imagination can creatively design new fears for the future. Just as keeping adolescents busy helps them avoid mischief, **serving** others helps adults apply the same philosophy to themselves. In the long run, **serving** others saves us more time and trouble.

༄༅

STILLNESS-

As the only female among a five-male household, I'm realizing that I speak way too much, and everyone else listens way too little... a terrible combination. Trying to teach my sons to listen is a monumental task in and of itself, but isn't everyone guilty of forgetting the difference between "hearing" and "listening?" I'll be the first to admit that I was *that* student who anxiously held up my hand thinking about my amazing question, and I forgot to listen to the person right before me asking the same question.

Social media has exacerbated this problem because it poses as a huge canvas for monologues. I don't mean to bash social media, but I would love to see a better technology tool designed to facilitate true dialogue for growth instead of grumbling, unity instead of division, creativity rather than quarreling. I think we are missing the "smart" thing that will encourage us to listen to one another instead of simply talk until we are too blue to see our own faces in the script.

My eldest son once said that it'd be "really cool if we could hear God's voice." When I tried explaining that we can, I began to see the difficulty in this depiction. The root of the problem is that if we can't listen to others well, how can we possibly know how to be **still** and silent long enough to hear a **still**, small voice from Heaven.[42] I recall having the same desire to hear my maker's words aloud, but over the years, God gave me ample and beautiful opportunities to learn how to hear Him. Now, I want to continually learn to not simply hear Him, but also listen and obey. *"Before I was afflicted, I went astray, but now I obey your word"*.[43] Listening, like humility, is a lost art that the world, full of fancy one-liners, needs to rekindle and renew.

In addition to listening, we have to interact with the Word of Truth as we would in any other relationship or social media platform for that matter. Otherwise, praying and reading can become as mundane and rote as folding laundry. Humans were designed for intimate relationships, but "relationship" implies two parties interacting. We can't be the only person speaking all the time, or we risk forgetting what the other person's voice sounds like. A child will be spoon-fed as long as we never teach him to hold his own fork. Likewise, we have to learn to interact with God and listen to His voice through His word as we would with anyone else.

When my little Levi's developmental progress was slow as molasses, it would pain me to watch him struggle through every normal and otherwise automatic childhood development. He couldn't roll over regularly, he couldn't crawl naturally, and he walked flailing his arms around for extended balance. Once he was "trained" to suck out of a straw, he would struggle to chew. Fixing one area of his growth would delay another. I would try to address every potential issue, but sometimes I would wonder if he'd ever grow at all. Then I would be reminded that I had bought into the current state of *instant gratification thinking*. We aren't used to waiting for anything for more than five minutes. When a call or text is not responded to within seconds, we assume the worst— insensitivity, foul play, or even desertion. My sweet second son has an unusual knack for patience. He will have such a leg up on his peers when it comes to waiting for a response.

Similarly, our perceived "unanswered" questions in the stillness of night may just be addressed in a different manner than we imagined. When we wait for a green light from God by humbly sitting still until we get the nudge to move, we learn to hear him more clearly and correctly. Just as Noah sent out a dove more than once to be certain God was saying, "Now you may open the doors," we too may need to be silent for a time in order to rectify our restlessness, enjoy our **stillness**, and react accurately.

Such a **stillness** is commonly called *meditation* in both the secular and the biblical worlds. Whether compensating for our natural busyness or seeking some solace through yoga, pilates, stretching, or walking, in the end, we must learn to incorporate silent prayer in such a way that honors God and humbles our hearts. The world offers us options to slow down in order to find peace in ourselves, but ultimately, meditation is at the heart of all these practices, and we cannot be **still** and find lasting peace in ourselves alone. Apart from God, the momentary peace will fade when the physical practice ends. Lasting peace and longterm listening skills require God's voice and our silence. Hence his recommendation to "Be still and know that I AM GOD"[44] (emphasis added).

God even warns us how we approach Him lest our prayers become all about what we think is best. *"Do not be quick with your mouth, Do not be hasty in your heart to utter anything before God; God is in heaven and you are on earth, so let your words be few."*[45] Meditation by definition requires reflection or contemplation, which are both quiet acts. Because I am prone to talk more than I listen, I often re-read these words in hopes of hearing God accurately: "*May these words of my mouth and this meditation of my heart be pleasing in your sight, LORD, my Rock and my Redeemer.*"[46]

Be careful though: perfection amidst **saturation, service,** and **stillness** is never the goal, but the more I saturate, serve, and sit silently with God, the more I desire His kingdom above my own, giving me a **settled** heart and mind. Then, the more naturally I recognize the "red flags" of fear when they sneak up to steal my fearless heart. The more I'm growing with God and abiding in Christ, the more my life is free from anxiety.

8

Stress vs. Worry

"The greatest weapon against stress is our ability to choose one thought over another."

— William James

Ten minute massage? Good cup of coffee? Absolute quiet and stillness? There are many quick ways of relieving stress if we only have a few minutes, but in actuality, *stress* or call it *pressure*, NOT ANXIETY, is a man-made, completely avoidable phenomenon. Now of course among many of Jesus' promises of love, security and joy, there was also the promise that we will have hardship in this world. Illness, yes. Sadness, of course. Anger and frustration, without a doubt. These are all products of a broken world. But *stress*, no. I don't believe God ever meant for us to feel such a thing. That is why Jesus made the bold command in Matthew chapter six, "Do not be anxious [stressed] about your life," and why Paul later affirms this command in Philippians chapter four, "Do not be anxious about anything." If we are feeling those emotions as they are associated with *stress* and not godly concern, then something has gone wrong. Either we are unable to hear God's voice (**saturation** needed), we are taking on God's job for ourselves (**stillness** needed), or we are ignoring personal conviction (**service** needed).

Even so, comments from other people can affect our perceptions of ourselves and the world around us as easily as the food we eat affects our health, or the books we read affect our thoughts. Today "comments" are not just heard from a passerby, but screaming from the devices adhering to our hands. Camps and columns are dedicated to help people detox from our screen-filled society. Why then do people struggle to separate from their added appendages, knowing the stress they are stealthily creating?

When we are faced with the "scary unknowns" in life, *Google* is an easy escape to land our imaginations on for a time until a real answer proves trustworthy. Unfortunately the answers we receive from search engines create stressful "what ifs" that rarely prove true. Our imaginations have much more advantageous functions.

I remember all the times I fretted over my first born's "normal" issues, worrying and wondering about his own creative design, scouring the web for a finite solution to his problems. When there were too many possibilities to dissect, I would be left to pray. I prayed for the faith to trust and walk in the tired unknown. I prayed for the *perspective* to remember the little boys and little girls all over the world with serious medical problems. The moms and dads sitting at hospital bedsides instead of sitting around in boxes, playing imaginary race car games. Once little Levi came into the world, God granted me a new freedom from fear through the first-hand look into those lives being lived out in hospitals.

When my desire to create comfort for my kids overshadows my ability to play pretend with them, I've stepped into dangerous territory. Children sense frustration and feel fear. When we naturally forget *perspective*, we have to choose to redirect our own thoughts, just as we would redirect an ungrateful child's heart to see through another lense. We force our natural desire for comfort and ease to shift as we see how uncomfortable we could be on an even harder road than our own. Even if we are living out our days next to a sick baby, difficulty is all relative when we view it through the lens of harder trenches.

Praying for the right *perspective* is a prayer that God loves to answer, because He desires for us to view the world from His eyes, so that we might live at peace in the midst of brokenness. Just after Levi was born, some old friends of ours found out their son, who was about the same age as Levi, was diagnosed with a rare cancer that resulted in many rare surgeries. It was no mere coincidence that I ran into this brave mother preparing her son for brain surgery as my son was receiving his own double gastric surgery. God gave me a *perspective* shift opportunity as he apparently did for her as well. It is the divine appointments that keep us trusting God even when the world feels like it is crumbling around us. *"God is our refuge*

*and strength, an ever-present help in trouble. Therefore, we will not
fear, even if the mountains fall into the sea".*[47]

ഇൽൽ

Jesus didn't feel full of gratitude every moment of the day
because some moments were harder than others, but he
always knew how to abide because he was one with the Father.
Thus, when he came down to Earth, he perfected **saturation:**
listening, reading or reciting God's word in truth. He
promoted **service:** with a servant leader's heart, he lived for
His Father and others before himself. He practiced **stillness:**
regularly getting away to a mountain top to be alone with
God, walking along the water for a time until he rejoined his
friends, and rising early just to be alone with his Father. He
spent time recharging frequently despite all he could have
accomplished in a day, knowing how short his time on Earth
actually was. Even in all those disciplines, Jesus felt frustration
with the sin in those He loved. Just after his last supper, Jesus
began to prepare his heart for the hardest calling of all time:
    *"'My soul is overwhelmed with sorrow to the point of death.
Stay here and keep watch with me.' Going a little farther, he fell
with his face to the ground and prayed, 'My Father, if it is possible,
may this cup be taken from me. Yet not as I will, but as you will.'"*[48]
    Talk about a potentially anxiety-driven, stressful time.
Knowing he was about to suffer and die, Jesus grievously
reprimands his closest "brothers," who are fast asleep while he
is preparing for the cross. Anxiety emerges most often when
someone is most vulnerable. Exhaustion, illness, or loneliness
due to circumstances creates the perfect recipe for stress to

emerge. Jesus was up all night praying. He was physically alone as his friends slept with heavy eyes, and he was overwhelmed to the point he was sweating drops of blood. Even with all of these elements, *Jesus was not anxious*. Frustrated at sin, yes. But not stressed as we understand and feel it today. He never sinned; he merely abided with His father, and in doing so, trusted His will above all else. *"He will remain in perfect peace, He who remains steadfast because he trusts the Lord"*.[49] It is an unseen enemy that tempts us to feel alone and distrust our Creator, which creates additional anxiety and stress.

⊱✧⊰

I have learned to recognize the falsehoods creeping into my life when Satan tries to steal my joy with the anxiety and exhaustion of every-day life. I must make a choice, with the help of the Holy Spirit, to alter my *perspective*. My family and I have been through difficult times, so when normalcy starts causing stress, somehow I feel even more alone in the trenches. Once again I have to remind myself why Jesus had to die in the first place. Without his death, there would be no hope, and without his resurrection, there would be no healing or helper. Without my Bible, I would probably be covered with those previously mentioned "band-aids" or living with addictions in an asylum. *"Great peace have those who love your word, and nothing will make them stumble"*.[50] The truth is that we are never alone. Even when it appears that all his friends and family had abandoned Him, Jesus never felt alone. That is why he never felt stressed. When we stay close to our maker, we stay far from falsehood.

Losing many people I loved brought me to a place where I thought I had conquered all my fears. Yet I failed to see the many names worry wears. Worry has a way of warping. It camouflages and calls itself insurance. Insurance is a necessary part of increasing possessions. Those living near large bodies of water know full-well the weight of flood insurance. Money given ahead of storms helps lesson the load if and when the real hurricane hits. The future protection gives breathing room in the present uncertainties. The invention of insurance now seems invaluable, but when worry disguises itself as warranty, it is more destructive than a category four hurricane.

Are we still trying to pour all our preparedness into precautions? Canning, purchasing sand bags, and filling up gas cans gives off the impression of storing up for the next hurricane. In reality we are actually taking hours off of our lives. *"Who of you by worrying can add a single hour to his life?"*[51] I thought I ceased worrying because I didn't store up food and clothes or concern myself with having enough stuff. Trusting God's provisions in all areas of my life felt like a triumphant feat, so I must not have any unwarranted worries anymore. Wrong.

Jesus pointed his disciples away from the needless worry of having enough food and clothing, but I can still concern myself with day-to-day frustrations and concerns just as easily as the next person. I can store up cans of worry in a different manner, but the underlying issue is all the same. *I'm carrying concerns in such a way that I've lost perspective on life and lack trust in God.* I lose heart and carry a burden I was never intended to carry because I am human, I need a Savior, and because God wants to carry the burden for me. Only then can I help carry the burdens of others. The burden can be light if we let it go, and we must let it go over and over again. *It is a lifelong process of sanctification.*

At the core of every "stressful" situation exists two very simple, yet very significant problems: pride and fear. Fear can actually be traced to a symptom of pride, so in reality it's just one problem: people continually try their hand at headship because that is how sin originated. If we are scared of not having, we must take the reins so that we are not at a loss. If we can't "have the fruit" we must willingly decide to trust ourselves instead of God. We are fearful that we won't have enough of something, so we store up in our barns, our basements, or most recently our rental, air-conditioned storage units for a sad rainy day. We store up for a day that never comes, for a generation that doesn't want our "priceless" keepsakes. We store up in hopes it'll be worth something someday, but someday escapes us because regardless of a person's faith or beliefs, one fact is indisputable—every single person dies, and nothing tangible can be held after death.

We can trust in a greater purpose than storing up superfluous cans and sand bags though. While preparedness isn't wrong, there is a fine line between insurance and angst. We will never perfectly predict a hurricane's path because we are not in control of the weather. Likewise, we will never need to perfectly prepare for any other life disaster because we are not in control. God has ordered all things and a human cannot change God's plans or fully understand or anticipate them. Otherwise, we would in effect be God. The storms will come, and God will always prepare us for His good in His own perfect way. Dreams and sneak previews seem to be my preferred mode of rehearsal, but the feature presentation has always been in God's hands through my faith. It's a faith that comes only through trials by fire and storm. A faith that is much more precious than a perfectly planned day. Children who trust their parents enough to obey even though they don't understand all the details, unknowingly bless their own future. The same is true with God's adult children.

"But blessed is the one who trusts in the LORD, whose confidence is in him. They will be like a tree planted by the water that sends out its roots by the stream. It does not fear when heat comes; its leaves are always green. It has no worries in a year of drought and never fails to bear fruit."[52]

When worry is knocking at our doorstep because we are desperate for sleep, sanity, or security, we must revert back to those creative juices only we possess. We become like a child and play, trusting that tomorrow will come soon enough. Whether it's reading, running, gardening, golfing, or music-making, we must do something that requires us to imagine and stretch that creative muscle until we are sitting in a cardboard box (which is really not a box at all), like Antionette Portia's character in *Not a box;* we need to use our imaginations for good instead of "googling" ideas. The fun will dissipate the fear, and we'll recall the need to play in the middle of preparing.

More than that, if we can humble ourselves like a child, then God will graciously take away our worries and anxieties; but we still have to be an active part of the process. Good versus evil in our life narrative will always exist as it does in fictional narratives. Therefore, *"Humble yourself, under God's mighty hand, that he may lift you up in due time. Cast all your anxiety on him because he cares for you.* *Be alert and of sober mind, [because] your enemy the devil prowls around like a roaring lion looking for someone to devour."*[53] When we know the war is won, we can put on the right armor (**saturation, service, stillness**) to fight the battles here on earth, even those that disguise themselves as a third or fourth world war of worries.

9

Future Fears (red flag ready)

"Never be afraid to trust an unknown future to a known God."

— Corrie ten Boom

I was lying in bed sound asleep hoping to gain at least a few solid winks before welcoming our fourth child into the world early the next day. Something or someone creeped into my left inner ear and began slowly scratching at my ear drum. The annoyance woke me gradually like the brushing of hair from the wind. Before too long, my mind couldn't quiet itself at all. What started as a scratch soon transformed into a saga. I knew I must have something stuck in my ear, and it was turning into an infection. Within minutes I was sweaty, restless, and nauseous. Now I felt quite certain this would absolve my chances of actually keeping one of my children after giving birth because I would be too sick to care for him. As I was on the verge of vomiting, a thought crossed my mind: *after all these years of peace in chaos, I am having a panic attack.* I hadn't had any panic problems for probably a decade, so why all of a sudden? In desperation, I interrupted my husband's last chance for a good night's sleep for a while, and I begged him to pray over me. Without hesitation, Matthew calmly requested that God take away my nausea, my discomfort, and my fear. In all honesty, within seconds I felt relaxed and could barely hear the scratching. My body temperature regulated, and I quickly felt healthy and calm, falling back to a peaceful sleep. The next morning after an early shower, I used a Q-tip and pulled out a piece of cotton that must have come loose in my ear the prior day during the same ritual. While there are many comical ways of looking at the situation, I present it from both a practical and spiritual perspective. No matter how secure we feel in any given moment, there is always evil looking for ways to dismantle our assurance. Our minds, especially when tired or tense, will play tricks on us if we don't possess the power of the Holy Spirit. In the midst of illness or in the middle of the night we must remember that reality isn't as close as it is during the day. We need words of wisdom, prayer partners, or texts of truth readily available to keep us from spiraling into a pandemic problem.

During widespread travesties like economic shutdowns and global pandemics, news headlines tend to heighten hysteria and hopelessness. For example, during the COVID Pandemic of 2020 news anchors fanned the flame of fear. A Cable News Network reporter reposted a podcast commentary from a former first lady involving her bout with mild depression during the pandemic: "A Census Bureau survey found that one in three Americans are reporting symptoms of depression or anxiety, more than three times the rate from a similar survey conducted in the first half of 2019. And because one of the best ways to fight coronavirus is through social distancing, people have gone long stretches of time without seeing their friends or family, exacerbating the already widespread problem of loneliness, which can be deeply harmful to one's mental health."[54] Healing from pandemics will come one way or another, just as death comes to us all, but how we handle the "aftermath" of a crisis situation determines our future. Holocaust survivors lived through hiding, hurt, and horrors, yet like many prisoners, they kept going because they lived in hope. A crisis or pandemic always feels new and unprecedented, but it is no different from the heart of war that has come to many throughout history. There is nothing new under the sun.[55] When we prepare our hearts for the unknown, we don't return to slavery because we have become a person of freedom in our rightful identity. The walls of isolation around us don't determine our hope. Rather, what we do during those days behind walls determines the outcome.

The Spirit you received does not make you slaves, so that you live in fear again; rather, the Spirit you received brought about your adoption to sonship. And by him we cry, "Abba, Father." The Spirit himself testifies with our spirit that we are God's children."[56]

Few people can sit in a cell for an extended period of time without coming out changed—some for better, and some for worse. We can return to a life of slavery even after we are granted freedom. We "relapse" so to speak through familiar chains: a slave chained to our computer, our health, our bank account, or simply a slave to anxiety and fear.

Some people never let go of their bitter roots, refusing to change their chains and expecting the world to become better without their own introspection. Often if we look closely at ourselves, we will feel pain or stings that require medical (and spiritual) attention, yet that sting means the medicine is cleaning the wound. Without pain, we wouldn't know when to run from fire. We may keep sitting in our prison cell long after it was time to walk out.

Still, without a secured future, we may begin to wander aimlessly. Even the well-known wanderer from *Into the Wild*, Christopher McCandless, kept a detailed journal in order to document days and dictate details for a sense of rhythm and routine. He was a searching soul desirous of spontaneity, flexibility, and freedom to eradicate societal norms. I'm in accord with his love of flexibility and spontaneity, but there are many people who are not prone to prioritize or prepare unless demanded by a paycheck or parent. Thus, a COVID-kind of quarantine will shake their emotions because such individuals do not recognize their need for boundaries or anchors. We have to be "red-flag" ready to avoid running back to slavery. If salvation is eternally secure, why are there people who seem to "fall away from faith" in our society? There are dimensions and discussions there that are too lengthy and in-depth to cover here. The important thing is to own our part in the growth process so that apathy doesn't set into our bones and open the door for another panic attack.

When I first starting having children, I recall someone telling me that the second I felt like I had the hang of things, they would quickly change, keeping me on my toes (and knees). While this is true for most kids, our super-early, super-strong, Levi Joe didn't come with the same patterns as standard children. We sometimes say he has "specialties" when describing him to strangers, but this doesn't accurately define his personality or personal differences. Levi isn't a "special needs" child in the way our society would understand that label, but his specialties simply require a degree of study that exists only through constant relational exposure. Take his sleep cycles for instance. Sometimes Levi wants to mummify himself in his covers until he falls asleep and can wake up fully soaked to the bone from sweat. Sometimes he wants to smash the right side of his body into the side of an armchair in order to relax and fall asleep (much like he was positioned in utero). Other times he prefers laying on the hard floor with no pillows, no blankets and nothing but a book under his arm in order to rest easily. We constantly ask Levi to do things that we think will benefit his overall strength and comfort, but often times the things we think are useful for him are actually, in his opinion, quite unpleasant. It reminds me of the old movie *Cast Away*: after years of sleeping on the hard beach floor, Tom Hanks' character is uncomfortable when he finally receives a soft bed after his rescue. He tosses and turns until he resorts to sleeping on the hard floor in peace and tranquility. He had to relegate himself to what felt comfortable to him, not his surroundings.

My eldest son was just asking me about the difference between "fact" and "opinion," and it was difficult for him to see that some things that seem like facts are, in fact, (*pun intended*), opinions. For example, beds are comfortable—fact or opinion? Levi and Tom Hanks may disagree with our facts. I believe it is a "fact" that all humans desire a certain level of physical and emotional comfort. However, the mode of comfort is subjective. Recently, I heard a pastor speak about the importance of stepping outside our "comfort" zones in order to reach people around the country and the world with the truth of the gospel. However, stepping outside what is natural and comfortable looks different for everyone. Getting up at five in the morning is very natural for some and very uncomfortable for others. Eating dinner on the floor is normal in some cultures and horrifying to others. Raising four boys makes some people shudder and others jump for joy.

The point is that we have to constantly evaluate whether we are living in a state of ritual comfort that numbs us to the changes that God may require for our growth. Without "working out our salvation with fear and trembling,"[57] we'll return to being "slaves to fear." On the other hand, if we can begin to force ourselves to be somewhat uncomfortable, then we achieve new lenses of accuracy. In other words, when we are accustomed to calling scraps of metal, precious gold, then we miss out on the treasures actually in existence. A little discomfort also helps us to recalibrate our focus and decrease our pride.

I would never want my discomfort in raising four little boys to be compared with that of a mother who has had twelve babies in the African Sahara. Likewise, we cannot judge others for not living our same lives. No one is the perfect judge, nor does anyone have an equal estimation for growth requirements. In the same way that little Levi was never "high enough on the growth chart" when compared to kids in America, he looked perfectly healthy when compared to starving children around the world. We have to desire God's will above our own so that we respond well to life's challenges, which keep us on the right path and right growth chart.

"*Search me God and know my heart. Test me and know my anxious thoughts. See if there is any offensive way in me and lead me in the way everlasting*".[58]

Personal introspection is key to proper vision and proper growth. That way we avoid pitfalls because we see the red flags of fear creeping into our blind spots. We must focus on becoming more like Christ, not becoming more comfortable with your surroundings because those will constantly change as we grow, but without growth, we can easily slide backwards into familiar anxious thinking.

Anne Graham Lotz wrote about how humans grow similar to trees in their strength and endurance as juxtaposed with their hardships. She said,

> *When I was growing up in the mountains of North Carolina, every Sunday afternoon, weather permitting, my parents, my siblings, and I would go hiking. Inevitably, our climbs would take us to the ridge where the trees were so enormous we could all hold hands and still not be able to encircle the trunks. When I asked my mother why the trees were so much larger on the ridge than anywhere else, she replied that it was because the winds were the strongest and the storms were the fiercest on the ridge. With nothing to shelter the trees from the full brunt of nature's wrath, they either broke and fell, or they became incredibly strong and resilient.*

God plants you and me in our faith as tender
saplings then grows us up into "trees of righteousness,"
using the elements of adversity to make us strong.
And He leads us to endure, not just somehow, but
triumphantly as we choose to praise Him, regardless
of the storms swirling within us or the winds howling
outside of us.[59]

Lotz learned the value of resiliency. Facing fears and growing with God grant you fearlessness. Then you can become someone that, "is clothed with strength and dignity; [you] can laugh at the days to come."[60] There is no fear of the future, no fear of bad news, and no fear of failing to finish well. Having an unexpected panic attack ten years after my fears had subsided gave me additional humility to trust God's power through prayer. I don't have to fear another attack because I have learned through the grace of God to **settle** my thoughts should any resurface. I can rest assured that there is One who stays up throughout the night and never leaves my side.

10
Finishing Fearless

"I never think of the future - it comes soon enough."
— Albert Einstein

The milk spilled over the top of Levi's feeding-tube bag as I tiredly tried to refill it before breakfast. Milk spilled shortly after that when my oldest son attempted to fill his own cereal bowl. Milk also spilled hours later as I screamed at the sight of ants surrounding our kitchen table; they must have smelled remnants of the old milk spilled earlier. The day would come to a close with the largest spill of milk all over our garage because the grocery bag attendant didn't know I'd open the trunk so quickly allowing two gallons of milk to smack the floor and crack open simultaneously. Now that we were officially out of milk, I was actually relieved.

Spills happen in life, but they seem to happen a lot more when you try earnestly to avoid them. Frustration is my natural reaction to spills because I'm a relative neat freak, but after all those spills in 2015, and the last one filling our garage with that sour stench, I just laughed (especially because I decided to start buying the organic brand that day). Isn't this what I signed up for when I became a mom? If you can't handle spills, you shouldn't hang around kids. You have to be able to roll with the mess and allow the hiccups to strengthen your character. Children are always watching and learning how to respond themselves. Because God miraculously gave me so many children back to back, there wasn't much time to worry about life's messes.

My life, my story, is filled with messy details. Events that don't sound pretty or magical. Situations that took a long time to clean up. It can sound neat and tidy on paper, but the realities were hard and harried. Without them, though, I'd probably still be gripping someone's hand with sweaty palms fidgeting with a fake flower on my shirt. Aren't the spills the things that have taken away all the things that held me captive before? If we don't let the messes happen on their own, and try to enjoy the clean-up process, then they will just happen again, and again, and again, until we stop and laugh a little. When we try to keep our children from spilling anything in a vain attempt to keep ourselves from clean-up duty, we are ultimately hurting their chances of building true character while still under our roof.

Milk is really not that hard to clean up; it's nothing compared to a lifetime of messes. If we toil in vain to prevent potential disasters, we waste more years in stress than freedom.

If we toil for the safety of our independent children through "phone-finding" technology or extra "help" in their wallets, or if we toil to save every penny to put our kids through college or retire at a young age, or if we toil to salvage relationships that are broken and need time to heal, or if we toil to move up the corporate ladder, we toil in vain. We will find life to be akin to grasping wind. We are trying to control something that is not ours to hold, creating anxiety in the process.

"Have no fear of sudden disaster or of the ruin that overtakes the wicked, for the Lord will be at your side and will keep your foot from being snared".[61] There is reassurance in knowing that God is over everything and never leaves you. Fearing a sudden disaster only wastes the time you have today.

Before losing something sacred, our miscarried baby, I accepted a teaching position at a local college. I sought out this additional part-time job for the wrong reasons. I wanted to feel busy, have security, and establish my identity. However, deep down, I still desired God's will because I remembered desiring my own during my first engagement, and I lost my grip on truth. When we desire God's will above all else, rest assured, it will be done. *"This is the confidence we have in approaching God: that if we ask anything according to his will, he hears us. And if we know that he hears us—whatever we ask—we know that we have what we asked of him."*[62]

This was fulfilled in my own life. After the loss of our baby, my evening class was closed until the spring semester, but soon afterward I was pregnant with Levi. Something in me had changed, and I knew I needed to reject the job when it became available again. Shortly after declining the prestigious position, Levi came into the world, twelve weeks early, and I became a full-time mom. Surprisingly, I was not really anxious about my ability to care for Levi, or about Levi's future despite all the unknowns, but when I sat down and thought about it, I was anxious about losing my own life.

Everyone to some degree worries about "losing" his/her life. Some people avoid faith because of this concern, while others avoid marriage and children for the very same reasons. Either way, it's a last ditch effort in wanting to maintain our control over what we assume is the best way to live our lives. Levi's eventual departure from the hospital turned our neatly organized routine into a tailspin. I knew that it was easy to create new routines, but it was a lifestyle change that I had not anticipated.

God faithfully whispered as I opened up my Bible to find my footing that day, and read: *"Whoever finds their life will lose it, and whoever loses their life for my sake will find it."*[63]

What if we don't realize that by "losing" our old life multiple times means we will finally find the life we were meant to live. It's like when parents tell their children, "You'll thank me one day" as they complain about sharing their favorite treat. The child thinks that the cotton candy he's eating should be the only food he ever consumes because there isn't anything better out there. Not only are there better desserts than cotton candy, but eating it every day for the rest of his life would do so much more harm than good.

As I willingly let go of my cotton candy life, I gained a new *perspective* that shaped my attitude about my future trials. After Levi came home, and I lost my best friend in an unexpected tragedy, all my restlessness evaporated. Restlessness that had persisted due to too much time to think on the wrong things.

A new contentment ensued in my life: simplicity reigned with a sense of calm in stillness. Security for eternity held me captive, and my identity rested in Christ alone, not where I fit into the world's puzzle. Because I was repeatedly reminded of life's fragility, my fears vanished, and a lack of fear led to freedom and peace. However, there have also been moments since all the trauma that have made me ponder my position and posture.

Everyone has an innate desire to feel loved and needed. I don't think anyone would argue with that fact. Deep down it's how we were created. When we feel unloved or unimportant, that's when we begin to feel worthless and lifeless. I think our ever-growing use of the exclamation point via electronic communication pinpoints our desire to make everything and everyone feel important. I had high school students who thought it was appropriate to put this end marker after almost every sentence because they felt it was an "important sentence," instead of using it as it's intended: to exclaim with gusto!

It is easier to feel like our life matters when we are doing something that the world views as important. A military post, missionary role, or mega million-dollar investor all fall into the category of important positions. People pour their lives into different titles and achievements in order to feel important, but when our life's work isn't glamorous, envied, or admired it's easy to forget our importance. I don't think the desire to feel important is wrong. God made humans that way because He wants them to know their importance lies internally. He wants to satisfy our every desire. However, the day-to-day grind of an "average" existence can slowly wear down our definition of important. For that reason, turmoil, hardship, or even "spilled milk" along our planned route begins to feel like an infinite blessing or burden, depending on our choice of lens, because they reroute our focus. Should we choose the blessing, we learn to remember the importance and significance of every little moment in our day. We become aware of the truly important matters of our fleeting life, and we trust that our life has a greater purpose than what we are doing. We praise God for making us capable of reaching new heights that we would never have known prior to that mountain we are climbing or valley we are trudging. Trials really become precious gifts if our *perspective* has shifted by the grace of God.

Not everyone likes the limelight though. Not everyone enjoys great attention, and not many people seek worldwide fame, but deep down, every single person holds a desire to be "known." Whether it's merely by a single significant other, or an entire city, we all want to be understood and loved for who we strive to portray. Social media has made "being someone" and "doing everything" much more covetous. It's the Oz behind the curtain—a facade we've created in our minds, which only disappoints after our striving ceases and the curtain opens.

If we buy into the notion that we must be "known" by the world, we will chase after our tails in single madness. Nonetheless, monotony can crowd our view of reality as well. There are moments that make the months worthwhile, and there are weeks that weary our means of existence. Either way, *seeking* a*ccolade strips spiritual armor like candy entices kids.* Our need to feel independent and worthy blinds us from the reality of ephemeral circumstances. When we know that a long car trip is about to end, we can wait another minute to use the restroom, but if we don't know when it's going to end, we begin to panic in desperation. If we see our current circumstance as short-term, then we can appreciate it all the more. In essence, we must continually confront the balance of not losing ourselves to our title or circumstances and not losing ourselves to our culture. We don't have to wait until the clock strikes midnight or the calendar year changes, though. As stated, God's mercies are new every day, and all we can do is open up dialogue with ourselves and others to see if it's the right time to make a change in our daily routine. We can't be afraid to change, but we can't be afraid to stay right where we are for the transient time set before us. Either way, **saturating** our minds with truth, **serving** others before ourselves, and **sitting** silently before an omniscient God will keep us on the right path rather than following someone else's "right" for us.

Change and growth should always accompany humility and wisdom. *"Have I not commanded you? Be strong and courageous. Do not be afraid [of the unknown]; do not be discouraged [by lies], for the LORD your God will be with you wherever you go [through all life's changes]."*[64] Designing other little gods to provide me with comfort always discouraged my growth with God. I struggled not to create idols out of other people. My comfort in the midst of hard challenges came from those I could see and touch. Such idolatry combined with ingrained pride has always been my most reoccurring sin that produced the most anxiety in my life.

It began with my parents (as it does with almost all children). I worshiped, adored, or sought to please them with everything in me. After recognizing my parents humanity, I began to transfer this idolization to friends and significant others. Even with the revelation of wrongly worshiping my husband prior to marriage, I have found that I still have the propensity to place people on pedestals and look to them to give me all the advice necessary to live on this Earth. Whether it's a reality television family or someone who has already gone to Heaven, we as flawed humans find comfort in following those that lead lives we hope to emulate. However, *every single person will fall short of our expectations.* No one can live up to such a standard, but that is exactly why God decided to become a human being. It's easier for us to idolize something we can see, so He chose to become one of us, to leave paradise and enter a broken world so that we would have the perfect person to worship. Even those that claim to be His followers will fall, but it is not up to us to live perfectly. It is up to us to seek to live like the only perfect one, Jesus—through knowing and living out truth in love and humility we will experience peace in brokenness, which creates fearless faith—the antidote to anxiety.

"Now may the Lord of peace himself give you peace at all times and in every way. The Lord be with all of you."[65]

Notes

1 Philippians 4:8
2 Philippians 4:7
3 Keffer, Lindy. "Absolute Truth in a Relativistic World," Focus on the Family. Originally titled "Ultimate Truth: Discovering Absolutes in a 'Whatever' World." 1 April 2019, Copyright 2020. https://www.focusonthefamily.com/church/absolute-truth/ Accessed November 2020.
4 American Psychological Association 2020, https://www.apa.org/topics/anxiety/index Accessed 2020.
5 National Institute of Mental Health, "Anxiety Disorders" page, US department of Health and Human Services. https://www.nimh.nih.gov/health/topics/anxiety-disorders/index.shtml Accessed 2020.
6 National Institute of Mental Health, "Anxiety Disorders" page, US department of Health and Human Services. https://www.nimh.nih.gov/health/topics/anxiety-disorders/index.shtml Accessed 2020.
7 Anxiety and Depression Association of America, "Facts and Statistics" page. ADAA Founded in 1979. Copyright 2010-2020. https://adaa.org/about-adaa/press-room/

facts-statistics#:~:text=Anxiety%20disorders%20are%20the%20 most,of%20those%20suffering%20receive%20treatment. Accessed June 2020/

8   Platt, David. *Peace in the Middle of a Pandemic. Youtube* uploaded by *Radical* April 2020. [video] https://www.youtube.com/ watch?v=zd_4TBAIN8M

9   Philippians 2 and 2 Corinthians 11

10 Proverbs 12:25

11 Whippman, Ruth. *Tell Me What You See: The Rorschach Test and Its Inventor, The New York Times,* 14 March 2017. https://www. nytimes.com/2017/03/14/books/review/the-inkblots-hermann-rorschach-biography-damion-searls.html https://gospelinlife.com/downloads/the-dream-of-the-kingdom-5186/ Accessed July 2020.

12 Psalm 94:19

13 Proverbs 23:7

14 2 Peter 3:8

15 2 Cor. 10:5

16 Keller, Tim. *Daniel: Living by Faith in a Secular World.* MP3 sermon product by *Gospel in Life.* 30 April 2000. https:// gospelinlife.com/downloads/the-dream-of-the-kingdom-5186/ Accessed July 2020.

17 James 1:2-4

18 1 John 4:18

19 Psalm 119:71

20 1 Peter 1:7

21 Chambers, Oswald. *The Golden Book of Oswald Chambers, My Utmost for His Highest,* Dodd, Mead, 1953, 1993 ed.

22 John 14:27

23 1 Peter 1:6-7

24 Karr, Reid. "The Night that Took my Wife." *Desiring God*, May 2019. https://www.desiringgod.org/articles/the-night-that-took-my-wife Accessed 2020.

25 Lamentations 3

26 Ecclesiastes 3:14

27 2 Corinthians 10:5

28 Isaiah 41:10

29 Psalm 119:147

30 2 Timothy 1:7

31 "Working Later in Life Can Pay off in More Than Just Income," *Harvard Health Letter*, Harvard Medical School, Harvard Health Publishing, June 2018. https://www.health.harvard.edu/staying-healthy/working-later-in-life-can-pay-off-in-more-than-just-income. Accessed 2020.

32 1 Timothy 5:13

33 1 Thessalonians 4:11

34 Reinke, Tony. *Competing Spectacles: Treasuring Christ in the Media Age*, page 134. Crossway, 2019.

35 Harris, Tristan. *The Social Dilemma, Netflix Film* by Jeff Orlowski, 2020.

36 O'Neil, Cathy. *The Social Dilemma, Netflix Film* by Jeff Orlowski, 2020.

37 John 8:31-32

38 Psalm 107:20

39 Philippians 4:8

40 Myer, Joyce, *Battlefield of the Mind. 56*, Hachette Book Group Inc. 2015.

41 Proverbs 4:23

42 1 Kings 19:12

43 Psalm 119:67

44 Psalm 46:10

45 Ecclesiastes 5:2

46 Psalm 19:14

47 Psalm 46:1-2

48 Matthew 26:38-39

49 Isaiah 26:3

50 Psalm 119:165

51 Luke 12:25

52 Jeremiah 17:7-8

53 1 Peter 5:6-8

54 Gordon, Allison. "Michelle Obama says she's suffering from 'low-grade depression'" Cable News Network, A WarnerMedia Company. 6 August 2020. https://www.cnn.com/2020/08/06/us/michelle-obama-coronavirus-depression-trnd/index.html Accessed 2020.

55 Ecclesiastes 1:9

56 Romans 8:15-16

57 Philippians 2:12

58 Psalm 139:23-34

59 Lotz, Anne Graham. "Tree of Righteousness" *Joy of My Heart Daily Devotional, AnGeL Ministries.* Copyright 2020. All rights reserved. annegrahamlotz.org

60 Proverbs 31:25

61 Proverbs 3:25-26

62 1 John 5:14-15

63 Matthew 10:39

64 Joshua 1:9

65 2 Thessalonians 3:16

About the Author

As a child, I concerned myself with too many cares to count, mostly for the sake of control and fear of the future.

As more and more of my fears came to fruition, I was struck with the oxymoronic truth: peace in the midst of chaos comes from giving up control and gaining fearlessness. I am a creative, organized creature, married by the grace of God to a grace-giving man. We have defied odds in our relationship and are miraculously raising four little boys.

I continue to live out oxymoronic contradictions daily. As a former English teacher and lover of words, I have blogged for a decade while ignoring basic grammatical rules. Educated in public universities, taught in private, and now I am homeschooling my own. Words have always been important to me.

Quiet words become inspirational stories that change lives. Because the world can be a bit loud, we all need to share tools to simplify and create peace in the chaos. I continue to share at http://carefullycareless.org.